CROSS TRA
REINING, CUTTII

BY RICHARD E. "RICK" DENNIS

FIRST EDITION

EDITED AND PUBLISHED BY
GLORY ANN KURTZ
P. O. BOX 1397
BOYD TEXAS 76023

COVER DESIGN BY AYSHA HOFFMAN

COPYRIGHT BY RICHARD E. "RICK" DENNIS
2012 - ALL RIGHTS RESERVED
ISBN 978-0-9720477-1-5

FOR ORDERS AND INFORMATION, CONTACT RICHARD E. DENNIS, WIND RIVER COMPANY LLC, 701 CARNATION AVE., METAIRIE, LA 70001 (985) 630-3500.

E-MAIL: WINDRIVERCOMPANYLLC@YAHOO.COM
WEBSITE: HTTP://WWW.WINDRIVERCOMPANYLLC.COM

ABOUT THE AUTHOR

R ichard E. "Rick" Dennis was born in Birmingham, Alabama. His resume' spans 44 years from 1969 to the present and includes: serving in the United States Army during the Viet Nam War, a Drug Enforcement Special Agent, a Certified Police K-9 Instructor/Trainer and a private sector business professional. His private-sector business specialties include: security consultation, drug and alcohol interdiction specialist, risk analyst and professional reined cow horse trainer.

Dual Train and Rick Dennis showing in the National Reined Cow Horse Association (NRCHA) Derby, Medford, Oregon, in the Herd Work. Dual Train is a 1995 AQHA sorrel mare by Dual Peppy out of Nics Train by Reminic.

In 1990 the author's equestrian career began with the purchase of a team penning and team sorting horse that was a precursor to an adjunct business, as well as his next career

2

as a professional horseman, Quarter Horse breeder and professional reined cow horse trainer. In 1997 Rick saw his first cow horse class while competing in a team sorting in Murfreesboro, Tennessee. The author thought this was the most exciting equestrian event he ever witnessed in the performance horse arena and decided to specialize in this event.

Rick's quest for a reined cow horse, or a stock horse as they're commonly referred to, landed him at the prestigious and legendary Ward Ranch in Tulare, California. His first trip to the ranch was in 1998 where he met the legendary California icon, NRCHA Hall of Fame inductee and Quarter Horse breeder Greg Ward. The author's motto is, "If you want to be the best, you have to learn from the best and compete with the best" and as far as he was concerned, he arrived at the best place to learn the "Art of The Reined Cow Horse," the best place to compete, the West Coast NRCHA shows and the best place to find his first reined cow horse prospect.

While at the ranch, Rick learned Greg was battling his second bout with cancer and was impressed and amazed with the gutsy, no-quit personality of this legendary California reined cow horse trainer. During this trip, the author learned the true meaning of professional horsemanship, horse training and the athletic capabilities of the reined cow horse. He also met what would turn out to be his first reined cow horse purchase Dual Train, a 1995 AQHA sorrel mare by Dual Peppy out of Nics Train by Reminic.

Even while battling cancer, Greg was still training horses on a daily basis. Shortly after winning the 1998 NRCHA Open Snaffle Bit Futurity on Reminics Pep, Greg died from his illness that "ended his life but not his legacy as a California icon." Dual Train and Reminics Pep would be the last horses trained by Greg. Dual Train won the non-pro division of the Paso Robles, California Snaffle Bit

3

Futurity and was a finalist in the 1998 NRCHA Snaffle Bit Futurity, establishing the highest scores in the herd work (similar to cutting) and the fence work (a cow horse event).

The author recalls the real irony of the 1998 NRCHA Snaffle Bit Futurity being that Greg Ward gave each competitor a lesson in the properly trained reined cow horse: how to exhibit the rein cow horse in competition and the integrity of this California icon and why he was deservedly referred to as the "Master" in the reined cow horse industry.

After the Futurity and in 1999, the author purchased Dual Train and later a stallion Nic Chex from the Ward Ranch. For the next three years, Rick traveled from Louisiana to the Ward Ranch to ride, show and learn the fine art of training and "Mastering The Art of The Reined Cow Horse." In 1999 Rick established the first reined cow horse training and breeding facility in Louisiana and turned Pro in 2000. Since turning Pro, he has been training reined cow horses and teaching students in the art of "Cross Training 101; Reining, Cutting and Cow Horse," by personal instruction, the Internet and clinics in the U.S. and Europe with remarkable success.

To date, the author's stock or students have won world, national and state titles, money earnings and championships with the American Quarter Horse Association, American Paint Horse Association, National Reined Cow Horse Association, National Cutting Horse Association, American Cutting Horse Association, National Barrel Horse Association, National Stock Horse Association, Louisiana Stock Horse Association and the National Reining Horse Association in reining, cutting, cow horse, team penning, team sorting and barrel racing.

The author contributes his success in the reined cow horse industry directly to his association with this legendary training facility in California, the California

4

stock horse, the many lessons learned from the trainers there and his personal affiliation with the other legendary reined cow horse trainers who have devoted their life's work to carrying on and continuing the tradition of the reined cow horse, the vaquero and the historical lineage attached to this remarkable horse.

Rick's list of accomplishments in the reined cow horse industry, are many, including:

• First Louisiana horseman to travel to the Ward Ranch to learn the art of training and showing the reined cow horse,

• First Louisiana horseman to establish a complete reined cow horse breeding and training facility in Louisiana: The Wind River Ranch,

• First Louisiana horseman to import reined cow horse stock from the Ward Ranch, Tulare, California to Louisiana, and

• First Louisiana horseman to establish a National Reined Cow Horse Association NRCHA affiliate - The Southeast Reined Cow Horse Association.

On September 11, 2001, the author's training and showing career was temporarily suspended with the terrorist attack on the Twin Towers in New York City, New York. Rick's security profession, his oil and gas clients, as well as the newly formed Home Land Security, received precedence above all private matters in his life.

Today the Wind River Ranch carries on and continues the legacy of the reined cow horse by standing two stallions: Dualin Oak, a 1999 AQHA chestnut stallion sired by Mister Dual Pep out of Tessa Oak by Docs Oak and Dual N For Me, a 2006 AQHA sorrel stallion sired by

Dualin Oak out of Peppys Angel Telesis by Lenas Telesis by Doc Olena. These two stallions were trained and shown by Rick with each enjoying an enviable achievement record. The author trained Dualin Oak as a green-broke, 3-year-old and Dual N For Me as a 2-year-old.

Both of these outstanding stallions are direct descendants of the legendary Ward Ranch and West Coast stock horse genetics. Rick and Dualin Oak are the 2004 State Junior Cutting Champions for Louisiana and the leading Jr. Cutting Stallion for Mississippi, MSRHA/NRHA Open Green Horse Reining Champions as well as Champions and money earners in reining, cutting and cow horse in stock horse competition.

Dualin Oak is a World Show $3,000 Novice Horse Open Cutting finalist and money earner as well as the top-ranked 2009 Louisiana cow horse sire. Dualin Oak is a Champion and a sire of Champions and money earners!

Dual N For Me also carries on the Stock Horse tradition by being an AQHA Junior Reining Circuit Champion as well as a money earner and champion in reining, cutting and cow horse in stock horse competition.

Today, the author continues to train multiple event stock horses, work in the private business sector and enjoys being a freelance writer and author. He contributes training and educational articles for the on-line magazine www.allaboutcutting.com and authored his first book: *THE AMERICAN HORSE INDUSTRY, Avoiding The Pitfalls*, providing the equestrian enthusiast real lessons and insight in negotiating the pitfalls associated with the equestrian industry.

This book can be found on the Internet, in retail book outlets and on the author's website www.windrivercompanyllc.com.

PREFACE

*C*ross *Training 101, Reining, Cutting and Cow Horse* is the second book in a training series authored by Rick Dennis. The author is a professional reined cow horse trainer with over 20 years experience in the stock horse industry and an avid teacher of cross training reining, cutting and cow horses. His training methods teach a student and a horse to perform in these three separate equestrian disciplines, enabling the equestrian team to compete in the prestigious reined cow horse show arena.

The training and teaching methods used by the author were learned, developed and fine tuned during his expansive career in the reined cow horse industry both from personal showing and training experiences as well as by personal association and influence with the legendary and Hall of Fame West Coast stock horse trainers in the industry. From these personal experiences, his opinion is the reined cow horse or stock horse is the most exciting horse to watch in the performance arena, the most demanding to train, demonstrates extreme athletic ability, superior cow sense and is the true "King" of the performance horse industry.

This book brings the reader through the necessary steps in training the multiple-event performer or reined cow horse from colt breaking and starting under saddle to the finished cow horse in all training disciplines such as snaffle bit, bosal, two-rein and bridle. This continuous training represents years in a horse's life for each accomplished training discipline and spans approximately five years. With the proper training, the reined cow horse at seven years of age, is a finished bridle horse: finely tuned, light in the face and responding to the ever-so-soft gentle cues, whispers and direction of the rider.

There are many descriptive adjectives that could be used to describe the reined cow horse or stock horse but the two that come to the author's mind the most are "amazing" and "demanding."

John Ward showing Nic Chex in the Fence Work of the 2000 NRCHA Stallion Stakes. Photo by Leslie Day.

DEDICATION

This book is dedicated to the Vaquero (Spanish) cowboy, the Stock Horse or Reined Cow Horse, traditional Vaquero training methods: snaffle Bit, bosal, two-rein and bridle, as well as the men, women and associations that have devoted years to carry on and continue this remarkable legacy as well as this binding tradition in our American history.

Chelsi Guillory and Some Hot Chic, a 2002 bay mare by Master Remedy out of Colonels Hot Chic by Just Plain Colonel, are the Louisiana Stock Horse Association Triple Crown Champion: reining, cutting, cow horse, shown performing the herd work portion of the event.

ACKNOWLEDGMENTS

The author recognizes and acknowledges the following individuals for their contributions to *Cross Training 101, Reining, Cutting, Cow Horse* by the use of photographs taken by them and used in formulating this book:

- Midge Ames Photography.
- Circle H Photography.
- Dana Photography.
- Steve Sessions Photography.
- Steve Guitron, Custom Rawhide, Vista, CA
- Rhonda C. Hebert
- Gordon Hayes, GH Bits Of Silver
- The National Reined Cow Horse Association and Jay Winborn for the use of the NRCHA logo.

The author also recognizes and acknowledges the following individuals for their professional influence and contributions to the author's education in learning the art of professionally training, exhibiting and breeding the California Stock Horse or three event Reined Cow Horse:

- Greg Ward, Ward Ranch, Tulare, California - NRCHA Hall of Fame.
- John Ward, Ward Ranch, Tulare, California.
- Barney Skeleton, Skeleton Performance Horses.
- Teddy Robinson, Robinson Cow Horses - NRCHA Hall of Fame.
- Smokey Pritchett Cow Horses - NRCHA Hall of Fame.

ABOUT THE FRONT AND BACK COVERS

The front cover photo depicts Dual Train, a 1995 AQHA sorrel mare sired by Dual Peppy out of Nics Train by Reminic, being shown at the National Reined Cow Horse Association Hackamore Classic by John Ward, an NRCHA Million-Dollar Rider and two-time NRCHA Snaffle Bit Futurity World Champion.

John is the son of the legendary NRCHA and 2015 National Cutting Horse Association Riders Hall of Fame inductee Greg Ward. Dual Train is a 1998 NRCHA Snaffle bit Futurity finalist, NRCHA Superior Cow Horse, NRCHA Maturity Champion, Snaffle Bit Futurity Champion, AQHA Junior Cow Horse World qualifier and money earner in reining, cutting and cow horse.

The back cover photo depicts Nic Chex, a 1996 bay stallion sired by Reminic and out of Bueno Chex Kaweah by Bueno Chex being shown by John Ward at the Natioinal Reiined Cow Horse Association Pre-Futurity show at Paso Robles, California. Both horses were bred by and trained at the Ward Ranch, Tulare, Calif. Nic Chex is a 2000 NRCHA Open Reserve Stallion Stakes Champion, Open NRCHA Derby finalisst, 2000 Open Johnny quick Maturity Champion, 2001 NRCHA Hackamore Champion and an NRCHA Superior Cow Horse.

Both horses were bred and trained by the Ward Ranch, Inc., Tulare, California, owned by the author Rick Dennis and are the foundation stock of the first reined cow horse breeding and training facility in Louisiana, the Wind river Ranch, owned and operated by the author as well.

Both photos are by Midge Ames.

The above photograph depicts Greg Ward at the age of 62 with Don Dodge. Greg died of cancer in 1998 after winning the 1998 NRCHA Snaffle Bit Futurity astride Reminics Pep at the age of 63. Greg will be inducted into the NCHA Riders Hall Of Fame in 2015. Don Dodge is a member of both the NCHA Members And Riders Halls of Fame. Photo by Gordon Hayes.

12

TABLE OF CONTENTS

Page   **Chapter**

HISTORY OF THE REINED COW HORSE

The original stock horse name is a historic phrase as is cow horse or cow pony and is still used colloquially referring to a particularly small, agile, cattle-herding horse. It is a term that dates to 1874. Stock horses are characterized by their agility, quickness and powerful hindquarters and are usually noted for intelligence and "cow sense," having an instinctive understanding of how to respond to the movement of cattle so as to move livestock in a desired manner with minimal or no guidance from their rider.

These horses are used both as working animals on livestock ranches or stations and also in competition where horses and riders are evaluated on their ability to work cattle and perform reined work.

The long-standing history of the reined cow horse or stock horse has been traced and directly attributed to the Old Style or Vaquero (Spanish) training methods of the California and Southwest regions of the U.S. The California (Spanish) Vaquero's are credited with the development of these specific horse training styles and equipment which brought a horse along at a slow pace and ultimately produced a superior animal for use on the ranch to perform daily chores or working cattle.

It was this early lifestyle of the Spanish Vaquero's (Cowboys), their horses and specialized horse-training methods that eventually developed into competition on the Western ranches among Vaqueros and their horses. This century's-old training method provided him with his most prized possession and working partner: a Stock Horse that was light and collected, controlled with a whisper and yet exhibited the raw bone strength, speed, athleticism, heart and stamina to perform daily ranch duties, (i.e.) cattle herding, roping, calf separation, branding, fence building, range riding as well as general ranch duties.

14

The Gold Rush in California, modern livestock management and the Great Depression are the three major contributing factors in the decline of the Stock Horse in the early 19th and 20th centuries, which eliminated vast cattle herds and ranches. This realignment of economics caused the stock horse to become more of a luxury than a necessity and continued through World War II. There was little time to worry about the tradition of the Stock Horse, during these historical times, to prevent its legacy from slipping into obsolescence in our nations history.

At the end of World War II a group of California horse trainers came together to form the California Reined Cow Horse Association, in 1949, to preserve the legacy of the "Vaquero or Old Style" training methods and the California Stock Horse. This association eventually developed into the association we recognize today: The National Reined Cow Horse Association; established in 1988, and "Continues and Carry's On the tradition and legacy" of the remarkable Vaquero (Spanish) training traditions, the Reined Cow Horse and the Old West.

Reined Cow Horse Exhibition:
The three-phase events of a reined cow horse competition make it the most thrilling and demanding of all performance horse classes and tests the ability of both horse and rider. Horses are shown in classes by age and generally consist of a Futurity, a Derby, a hackamore or

15

bosal class, a two-rein or double bridle class and a bridle class for finished reined cow horses. Until lately, each class consisted of: Herd Work - similar to cutting, Reined Work and Cow Work - controlling a cow down the fence.

The types of classes offered are generally broken down by category and age of the horse (i.e.) snaffle bit horse show classes are reserved for the 3-year-old horses, derbys are reserved for 4-and-5-year old horses, including the Hackamore Classic that is reserved for the 5-year-old horse working in the bosal, two-rein or double-bridle classes are reserved for 6-year-old horses and the bridle spectaculars are reserved for finished bridle horse 7 years of age and over. The Stallion Stakes is another class offered for descendants of subscribed stallions in the industry.

The above photo depicts a legal bridle bit

Until recently, the three-event classes were required for all age groups to demonstrate the proficiency of the horse and rider performing in each type of training equipment such as snaffle bit, bosal, two-rein and bridle. Today, some classes only require exhibition in reined and cow work (controlling a cow down the fence). Each type of required training equipment coincides with the age of the horse. The snaffle bit is used on horses 3 and 4 years of age, the bosal is reserved for the 5 year olds, the two-rein or double bridle is used on horses 6 years of age and constitutes a small bosalito, or little bosal, spade bit with a roller and Vaquero bridle reins.

Each reined cow horse contestant is required to be in full Western regalia including Western hat, shirt, chaps and spurs.

CHAPTER 1

2-YEAR-OLD COLT BREAKING 101
FUNDAMENTALS OF BREAKING AND
STARTING A 2-YEAR-OLD

Blondys Dualin Oak (Dual Oak x Stella Peaches x Blondys Dude) as a 2-year-old, prior to being trained.

As January signals the beginning of a New Year, it's also the signal that it's the time when long-yearling horses, coming 2-year-old colts and fillies, are brought into the Wind River Ranch training facility to start training. I start accepting colts and fillies for breaking and starting during January of their 2-year-old year no matter what month they were born in, as that signifies their 2-year-old birth date.

One of the most often-asked questions I receive is, "How old should a young horse be before training begins?"

This single question has a myriad of meanings and answers. Training can be interpreted as imprinting at birth, halter breaking at an early age, teaching the yearling to lead, teaching it to pick its feet up as well as washing and grooming.

I refer to this type of human interaction as simply, "Getting to know your horse and your horse getting to know you." This early-age, hands-on affiliation definitely is a step in the right direction in preparation for future training, either by you or sending the youngster off to a trainer.

The real training begins when the young horse comes into the barn for breaking and starting under saddle. Quite often I receive horses for breaking and starting that were simply left to grow up in a pasture with minimal human contact since birth. These are the horses requiring the most effort and time spent from a trainer.

Any pre-training and handling the breeder can accomplish by his or her self prior to either initiating training or sending the horse off for training is a great help and a step in the right direction.

Safety

I cannot over emphasize SAFETY as being a key component for the do-it-yourself practitioner to practice on a constant and daily basis when dealing with young horses in a training environment. Even though they're babies, young horses are physically stronger than their human counterpart and your transitioning the young horse from a carefree, do-what-it-wants environment to a controlled working environment that is totally alien to them, can compromise your safety.

One of the basic concepts the trainer has to overcome is the horse's inherited flight-for-life instinct, which it enables when it fears something or becomes confused about a subject matter or training stimulus. The three components to training a horse involve the psychology of the PRP stimulus concept: Patience, Repetition and Praise. In the end, the owner should want a horse that works out of love and freewill rather than fear. Trust and respect are the most fragile components between horse, horse owner and trainer.

As a professional trainer, I can't overemphasize the training, as well as the training methodologies the young horse receives during this developmental period, is the foundation that will remain with the horse for the rest of its life. So take your training slow and easy and develop a working partner you'll be proud to own, ride and compete with.

Step 1 – Arrival At The Barn

Once the young horses arrive at the barn, each one is assigned a stall. Colts are opposite of the fillies. On the front of the stall is a placard indicating the name of the horse, owner's name, individual's name in charge of the horse, sex, veterinarian, emergency phone number and insurance papers.

I require every horse in training to have medical insurance. As my veterinarian once told me, "A horse is an accident waiting for some place to happen." In the slot on the back of the placard is a slip for insertion of a current medical record for the horse, current Coggins test and the last date they were wormed. Without a current health certificate, entry is not allowed.

Horse owners should be aware that horses are horses and no matter how much care a trainer provides them, a horse in a training environment can receive an injury from something as simple as taking a bad step in the training arena. I had a horse receive an injury – a cut – in a stall with no visible signs of how the injury occurred, which absolutely baffled me!

I require each owner to provide me with enough individual feed to properly transfer the horse from its present feed to the feed the barn is feeding. This precaution is used to reduce the risk of colic. If a horse is identified as a special-needs individual for medical reasons, the owner is required to supply this feed in addition to the specified and agreed-upon monthly training fee. I highly recommend a quality feed fortified with sufficient vitamins and minerals to sustain the young horse during training but also for natural growth while in training.

Step 2 – Training Begins

I generally give the young horses about two days to acclimate to the barn. Young horses coming in for training are not accustomed to the noise and daily goings on in the barn and this time period provides them with ample opportunity to settle in.

After the horses settle in, I begin to visit with the young horses on a daily basis and evaluate each one, writing my evaluation down. This is used to devise the best plan to proceed with training.

Each horse should have arrived with a halter. I eventually replace the arrival halter with a no-pull halter that is used to stop or prevent the young horse from pulling back. This type of halter is an ingenious device which uses a lanyard fitted at the rear of the halter, positioned on the back of the horse's ears with a pull ring on the bottom, that simply allows the lanyard to apply pressure behind the ears of the horse when the horse pulls back against the lead rope without warning or unnecessarily.

This type of halter is humane and is used on young horses that have a bad habit of pulling back and sitting down when tied up, which could cause injury to the horse. This type of halter is also designed to prevent injury to the

21

young horse by minimizing the amount of pressure being applied to the horse's neck and back as opposed to it pulling back against a stationary or fixed object such as a fence post, wash rack or breaking pole. When the proper halter is attached to each horse, I leave about two feet of the lead rope attached to the halter, which makes catching the young horse easier to begin its actual training.

The above "Be-Nice halter" is an example of a no-pull halter that will stop or prevent the young horse from pulling back.

An ample supply of hay is always available in the young horse's stall to reduce stress. This hay replenishing also accustoms the young horse to individuals coming in and out of its stall, which aids in its acclimation to human contact and stall cleaning.

Each day the young horse is visited in its stall by the trainer or assistant trainer. The lead rope is caught and the young horse is accustomed to being caught and handled. This is repeated on a daily basis until the short lead rope can be replaced by a normal sized lead rope and the young horse can be caught and led around freely in its stall area by the trainer.

Blondys Dualin Oak being shown at halter as a 2-year-old by Melissa Wickham.

One valuable lesson I've learned is that it's easier on the horse to start the initial handling process in the horse's stall where it's in a secure environment. Each one of my stalls has a tether metal ring attached to the wall that is used to teach the young horse to tie up properly. I begin the process by attaching a normal lead rope to the horse's halter and run the end of the lead rope through the tether ring with the off-piece in my hand.

I begin applying pressure on the lead rope end while gently coaxing the young horse to come to me while taking up slack in the lead rope with each forward step of the horse.

When the young horse arrives at the designated location, I maintain pressure on the lead rope with my hand, all the while talking to the horse in a gentle voice and rubbing my off hand all over the horse's neck, head and back.

If the young horse pulls back, I control the amount of pressure on the lead rope to attempt to stop the back up. If I can't stop the back up with hand pressure, I simply release the lead rope and repeat the process until a normal standstill is accomplished. Once the horse reaches the point where it can be tied up effectively, I begin the process of picking up a hoof and repeat it until I can pick up each hoof, handle it without much fuss and clean each hoof with a hoof pick.

The last training phase in the stall is grooming. By this time, the horse should tie up easily and have each hoof picked up and cleaned. When these two training phases are easily accomplished, I begin the grooming process using normal grooming instruments and repeat it until the entire grooming process is accomplished.

Step 3 – Walking and Leading

When I'm able to walk in the horse's stall, I attach a lead rope to the halter and lead the horse around in its own environment. The next training phase involves removing the horse from the stall at the end of a lead rope to begin training the horse to be led by a handler.

I generally enlist the aid of another individual to assist me in the initial leading process, simply because it's easier for two to lead a horse rather than a single individual. One should be in the front along side the horse and the other one should be in the back to coax the horse when necessary. This process is practiced on a daily basis until the horse can be walked and led around the training facility with ease by a single handler and the horse is following the handler relaxed and with a free will.

Daily, each horse is caught in the stall, tied to the tether ring, its hooves picked up and cleaned, groomed and taken on a daily walk, which reinforces the training you've established during this time period.

As an added extra phase of training, I instill in the young horses is that once I have them leading properly, I teach them to load and unload in a trailer. I use a simple two-horse slant load with a drop down door. I've learned it's easier on the horse to walk the filly or colt into a trailer rather than have to teach one to jump into a trailer.

Step 4 – Wash-Rack Training

One of the hardest phases of training is acclimating the horse to running water and the sound that it makes coming out of the hose as well as when its applied to the horse. For some reason, this sound simply scares some horses to death and they act as if a demon is coming after them. To overcome this flight-for-life inherited characteristic, I usually start the horse off standing next to me in the grass and not on the wash rack and just let it listen to the sound of the water coming out of the hose.

If the horse doesn't exhibit a violent reaction to the hose, I start the water application with a soft mist on the feet of the horse while watching the reaction of the animal in relation to the application. Once the horse is accustomed to the mist on its feet, I move up to the legs and so on until I can reach the back and the neck. If at some point the horse exhibits an adverse reaction in relation to water being placed on a particular portion of its body, I simply stop the process and repeat it until the horse can overcome his fears. When this phase can be accomplished, I move the horse to

25

the wash rack.

Step 5 – The Farrier

The last phase of the initial training process, prior to saddling the horse, is hoof trimming by the farrier. This is very important to the young horse in order for it to maintain the proper balance in the round pen and prevent leg, hoof and tendon damage.

I use two processes for this endeavor: 1) If the young horse doesn't mind the farrier working on its feet, the work continues and 2) if a horse or horses fight the farrier, I simply reschedule the farrier for another day and enlist the aid of a veterinarian to assist in the hoof trimming process by sedating the horse in order to complete the process.

The veterinarian will normally use a sedative such as Dormosedan injectable that is a sedative and analgesic to facilitate minor surgical and diagnostic procedures in mature horses and yearlings. This is a humane practice and sometimes is the best process for the safety of the farrier as well as the horse.

This initial training phase should be accomplished in approximately 30 to 45 days.

CHAPTER 2

2-YEAR-OLD COLT BREAKING 101
ART OF THE ROUND PEN - LONGE-LINE
TRANSITIONS, WALK, JOG, LOPE

Rick Dennis and Dual N For Me in the Round Pen.

In the last chapter, "The Fundamentals of Breaking and

Starting a 2-Year-Old," I discussed the basics of colt breaking, beginning with bringing them into the training barn, which included halter breaking, teaching the youngster to tie to a fixed object, leading, grooming, trailer entry and exit, bathing and farrier work. If everything is on schedule with your colt or filly and you have accomplished the training requirements in the previous chapter, you're ready to bring the youngster(s) to the round pen and initiate the second phase of training: learning and teaching "The Art of The Round Pen."

On the other hand, if you haven't explicitly mastered "The Fundamentals of Breaking and Starting a 2-Year-Old," and you still can't execute the training steps included in this chapter, you should not engage or attempt this next phase of training. The psychology behind training an animal is that he or she learns in steps and phases and graduates from one training phase to the next – or building blocks, which simply means in human terminology, the training and education of an animal begins in elementary school and progresses at each one's ability and appointed time frame until the youngster graduates from college and the desired training goal is achieved by the trainer.

It's also important to understand when an animal begins to grasp the training stimulus provided by the trainer, the training process seems to move along very rapidly and smoothly until the desired effect is received. Experience has taught me to fully train a reining, cutting or cow horse, it takes a minimum of 18 months, i.e., if the horse can successfully complete the desired training discipline, and another 6 months to fully condition the horse to the show pen.

If your desire is to have a futurity horse, the time allotted would calculate out to be 12 months of the youngster's 2-year-old-year. Depending on the futurity scheduled, i.e. either October or November of its long 3-year-old year, this would allow either 10 or 11 additional months of training. Of course this training schedule is dependant on lay ups for injuries or other physiological issues which may occur, thus hampering, slowing down or completely stopping the training progress as well as the training schedule and how rapidly the horse is able to learn.

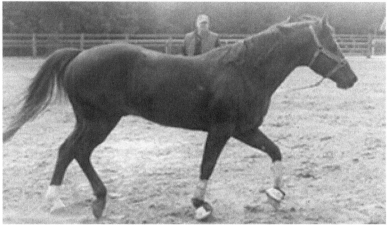

Rick working Dual N For Me on the longe line.

One of the main concerns an owner or trainer should completely understand is that animals mature on a different time schedule and it's more important at this training stage to be a "good Horse Listener" instead of a "Horse Whisperer," i.e., animals are genetically endowed with communication skills consisting of eye contact and various elements of body language. Therefore, it's more important for the owner or trainer to fully understand what the horse is trying to tell or convey to you by these genetically implanted signs of communication rather than trying to train a horse beyond its realm of comprehension, understanding or physical ability.

Essentially, the horse is going to dictate the training schedule and the training regimen each youngster requires to eventually reach the desired maturity and stamina level required to finish its training. As one legendary Reined Cow Horse Hall of Fame trainer once said, "A horse has to be trained in three phases: mentally, physically and spiritually." Another key element of training is to realize a performance horse is an athlete and requires a certain level of vitamins and minerals. Contrary to some popular training beliefs, I want my horses physically fit during training so each young horse in training matures at an optimum developmental stage by receiving a daily regimen of fortified feed complete with a vitamin and mineral pack such as Purina Omolene 200 14% feed.

This vitamin and mineral-rich fortified feed has always served me well. By no means should the reader interpret this statement as an endorsement of this brand of feed but merely an example of the type of performance feed I use, along with plenty of nutritious hay and salt, in both winter and summer. Other training facilities may use different types of feeds but over the years I've found this work's best for me in my geographical locations and training environment. A healthy and fit horse is more adept at receiving training than an under-nourished or out-of-shape horse. The main goal of nutrition is to allow the horse's body and muscles to rejuvenate after a training session and be ready for the next day's training regimen and arriving fit and fully alert.

Step 1: From the barn to the round pen

In preparation for the move from the barn to the round pen, I begin the next phase of training in the horse's stall. I add a regular halter over the no-pull halter and allow the youngster to carry the double halters around for a day or so. I then attach a shank or stud chain to the regular halter by running the stud chain through the outside ring of the halter, over the youngster's nose, through the outside ring and attach it to the top ring of the halter on the opposite side thus essentially attaching a nose chain.

Next I attach a regular lead rope to the no-pull halter and walk the youngster around the stall with the double lead ropes and the nose chain. If the youngster is intimidated by the nose chain or starts to pull back I simply allow the nose chain lead rope to go slack and control the youngster with the lead rope attached to the no-pull halter. I repeat this step as many times as necessary for the youngster to become accustomed to and familiar with the nose chain training aid.

The object of this training is to accustom the youngster to feeling another type of restraint. It will allow the trainer to control the young horse in the round pen to prevent injury, i.e., running into or up the round-pen wall, while negotiating the next phase of training.

One practice to avoid is snatching on the nose chain as a stimulus to make a horse negotiate a desired action which, on most occasions, will more often than not become problematic rather than a cure, i.e., pulling back violently, throwing its head in the air or rearing up instead of acquiring the desired action. If used properly, this training aid or apparatus is a humane and effective training tool that has been around and used for years to control studs as well as unruly horses.

In addition to the nose chain, I also introduce the youngster to safety gear: leg wraps and bell boots for the protection of legs, ligaments and heel bulbs. After the initial introduction, every horse is fitted with this safety gear prior to being removed from the stall for training in the round pen as well as other training phases. I initially start with polo wraps and eventually transition to splints and bells.

Remember, this initial phase of training is the most critical phase of a youngster's life and will be the foundation or developmental basis for future training and competition in the show pen. Therefore, complete trust is the desired bond between horse and trainer – not fear of the trainer or fear of specific training devices. Another

31

important goal is to produce a horse that is completely broke, a joy to ride and a barrel of fun to show in the show pen.

Step 2: Leading outside the round pen

When the youngster is able to be lead around the stall with the aid of the double lead rope and halter training devices with ease, it's time to remove the youngster from the stall and walk around the property. If the youngster becomes intimidated or unruly with the training apparatus, simply control it with the no-pull halter, accompanied by slight pressure from the nose chain. Repeat daily until the youngster can be lead around the property at will with ease and without mishap.

Step 3: Training in the round pen

Once the Step 2 phase of training is complete, it's time to bring the youngster up to the round-pen training area. I usually lead the youngster to the round pen with only with the aid of the lead rope attached to the no-pull halter and save the attachment of the nose chain training aid once I'm in the round pen.

When I arrive in the round pen, I usually walk the youngster around the round pen several times each way as an introduction. Remember, this is perhaps the first time the youngster has had the opportunity of being in a round pen so allow the youngster enough time to fully accustom itself to the new training environment before beginning the round-pen work.

If the youngster is not intimidated by the round-pen environment, I attach the nose chain and longe line and remove the lead rope attached to the no-pull halter. I then walk the youngster around the round pen a couple of times each way to allow the youngster to settle in.

Step 4 – Round pen preparation

In preparation of this training exercise, I've already placed a longe whip in the center of the round pen to aid me in initiating teaching and training the youngster to longe in this training area. I prefer a longe whip with a handle from 6 to 8 feet in length. I always instruct my students in the correct manner to use the round pen, the nose chain and the longe whip. The first item I teach a student is to fully understand the principles of the training aids, how each one works in relation to training and the most important aspect: preventing animal abuse.

The preferred goal is to introduce the youngster to another phase of training and training aid while not destroying the trust-bond established between horse and trainer during the previous training phase. I teach the student, and emphatically emphasize, that the longe whip should never be used as a source of punishment, to strike a horse from the nose, down its back and to the top tail area of the hip. Also, I teach the student never to strike a horse on the legs, which could severely damage tendons and ligaments. These are off-limit areas. Third, I teach the student the nose chain is designed to aid in the control of the horse and to prevent injury – not to punish the horse.

Step 5 – Teaching the horse to longe

When ready, I move the horse to the center of the training round pen and pick up the longe whip in one hand while holding the longe line in the off hand. I next take up a position alongside the horse for safety, which prevents the horse from bolting and running over you. I step to the rear of the horse while extending my off arm and hand, holding the longe line toward the head of the horse. Then I gently tap the horse square on the back rear hip or tail area to produce a forward motion of the horse out and away from me.

During this maneuver, be careful not to allow too much longe line to funnel through your hand, as this would allow

33

the youngster to end up close to or running into the round pen wall. One advantage the trainer can utilize is the horse's natural flight-for-life genetic makeup to aid in the training regimen. When a horse is presented with a training stimulus, it does not understand its natural instinct is to flee from the stimulus. So use this to your advantage.

While the youngster is trying to understand the training stimuli, but at the same time protecting itself from an event it doesn't understand, by kicking in the flight for life characteristic and moving away, this genetic inheritance is actually helping the trainer by causing the horse to move out and away from the trainer to initiate the longeing process which ultimately is the desired effect.

The purpose of the off-hand and arm extension is to allow the horse an escape route on a slack line. The initial reaction of the horse during this initial phase of training is to move off several yards, stop, turn and look at you as if to say, "What in the world are you doing?"

Once the youngster is moving out a short distance and stopping to turn and look at me, I walk to the side of the horse, move to the hip and repeat the exercise until the youngster learns to completely move around me without stopping. After several attempts and the youngster ends up too close to the round pen wall, I simply gather up the longe line and return to the center of the arena with the horse and start the exercise completely over again until the horse is moving freely and completely around me in one direction or another.

One important rule to remember is, "If the youngster is traveling to the left, the nose chain should be affixed through the ring on the left side of the face of the horse. If the horse is moving to the right, the nose chain should be affixed through the ring on the right side of the face of the horse."

I never attempt to change directions with a horse until the horse is moving freely around me when the longeing maneuver is initiated in one direction or the other – right or left. It doesn't matter if the horse is traveling at a walk, trot or lope. At this point, the desired effect to achieve is for the youngster to move around you in a relaxed manner and you're controlling the training exercise and building for the next training phase.

Step 6 – Teaching the horse to whoa or stop!

When the youngster moves out and away from me at will, the next training phase involves teaching the youngster to stop by voice commands and hand maneuvers. It doesn't matter if the youngster enters into a lope after being released by the trainer; the colt or filly will eventually slow down when it gets winded or tired. Just wait until this happens before attempting the "whoa" training maneuver.

When the youngster is moving freely and relaxed around me at a trot or a walk, I introduce the "whoa" or "stop" command. Simultaneously, I ask for the "whoa" and lift my arm up to engage the nose chain, which applies pressure to the nose area to aid in the stop. Never snatch the nose chain training aid to stop the horse. I keep repeating this training stimulus until the desired effect or "stop" is achieved. A rule to remember is the "whoa" should not be a sharp quick command but a long, drawn-out command in a deep but soothing voice.

The reason for the long, drawn-out command in a deep but soothing voice is this same type of command may be used by the rider or trainer in another training phase to complete a high-speed stop in a reining maneuver. The adverse effect of a sharp and quick "whoa" is that it normally causes the horse to stop on its front end with its head in the air which consequently results in a short stop instead of the desired long, flowing stop.

The desired effect for this training maneuver is for the trainer to enter the round pen with the horse, walk to the center of the pen, step to the hip of the horse, ask for the departure and the horse is longed around you freely against the round pen wall at will and stops fluid, smooth and correct on command.

Once I'm able to stop the horse on command, I walk to the horse to change directions. I never allow the horse to turn away from the wall and face me, as this will be problematic for another phase of training later on, i.e., round pen longeing without a halter. When I arrive at the horse's location I praise the horse, undo the nose chain and attach it to the opposite side of the horse's face, which is appropriate for the direction I'm looking for.

I next turn the horse in the desired direction, step to the rear of the horse and move the horse out and away from me, in the desired direction, while I maneuver myself to the center of the round pen to longe the horse in the opposite direction.

If during a directional maneuver the horse attempts to stop or slow down, I use a cluck and a whip pop to encourage the youngster to move forward. I never pop the whip toward the horse, strike or threaten the horse with the whip to encourage forward motion. This instills and encourages problematic training methods as well as an undesirable response from the horse.

Step 7 – Teaching the horse gate transitions: walk, jog and lope

During this next training phase we'll teach the youngster how to maneuver gate transitions: walk, jog and lope in the round pen. One important factor to remember is to fully warm the horse up in the round pen prior to initiating this important developmental training phase.

As a suggestion what I normally do is start the youngster in the middle of the training pen, step to the rear of the horse, move it out and away from me and just allow it to walk around the round pen training area. Next I coax

36

the horse into a jog and eventually a lope using a series of clucks and whip pops until the youngster is moving around the round pen in the desired manner. I allow the horse to continue at this pace until it slows down on its own. This initial warm up usually takes approximately five minutes to accomplish.

After the warm-up period, I allow the horse to walk around the round pen a couple of times to catch its breath and settle down. Afterwards I ask the horse to jog by using the cluck and whip pop. If the horse breaks into a lope, I stop the horse and begin the walk portion of the exercise and repeat until I can successfully move the horse from a walk to a jog without the animal breaking into a lope. Once I have the youngster successfully making this transition to the jog, I ask for a transition back down to a walk by using the verbal command "Easy" in a smooth, controlled and drawn-out manner.

I simultaneously use this verbal command in conjunction with raising my arm and applying slight nose pressure with the nose chain in order to facilitate this gate transition. When I'm able to successfully negotiate the horse from a walk to a jog and back down to a walk and a stop, then - and only then - do I add the final phase of this training exercise: transitioning the horse from a stop, to a walk, to a jog and into a lope, and then transitioning back down from a lope to a jog, to a walk, to a stop – all the while using verbal commands and hand cues.

Again, if this youngster is going to become a reining horse or a reined cow horse, this command is important to make fluid, smooth and correct transitions in the show pen while competing. This exercise should be practiced for approximately 20 to 30 minutes daily to reinforce the youngster's training, training proficiency and conditioning for readying the horse to the next phase of training.

CHAPTER 3

2-YEAR-OLD COLT BREAKING 101
ART OF THE ROUND PEN
FREE LONGEING, GROUND WORK,
BACKUPS, ROLLBACKS AND SADDLING

Rick longeing Dual N For Me, as a 2-year-old, in the round pen.

In Chapter 2, "Longe-Line Transitions For A 2-Year-Old," the proper training procedures were outlined to accomplish this training exercise as well as the training aids necessary to accomplish this phase of training.

If you can't hook your youngster up to a longe line in the round pen and successfully negotiate this training exercise, as well as stopping your horse with a verbal WHOA command, please do not attempt this next training regimen but instead return to the round pen and practice until you and your horse can successfully complete the required training outlined in Chapter 2.

Step 1:
At this point your horse should be able to negotiate the

longe line – walk, jog, lope transitions and WHOA with ease. Now the first thing I do is warm my horse up in the usual manner as outlined in Chapter 2 along with reinforcing the transitions in this phase of training.

After warm-up, I position the youngster on the wall of the round pen with the longe line and nose chain still attached. I next take up a position – along side, but at the head of the horse – to start teaching the youngster to back up and move off of pressure. In order to accomplish the backup while using the moving-off-of-pressure training phase, I incorporate the use of an English riding crop in my training exercises.

The first thing I do is to take up the slack out of the longe line. I roll it up and position it in my off hand, left or right, position my hand under the youngster's chin and apply backward pressure, which should bring the youngster's head down to move off the pressure. Next I ask for the backup using a technique where I apply backward pressure, release the pressure and re-apply the pressure until I receive a response – either positive or negative. If a negative response is received, such as failure to back up, I began tapping the youngster in the center of the chest with the riding crop.

After a few taps of the riding crop, while simultaneously applying pressure to the youngster's nose, and the youngster still won't move, I'll stop the exercise, walk the youngster forward to relax the horse, especially if it's showing signs of being pressured or becoming irritated with the training exercise. This directional training, or in simple terms, turning a negative response into a positive response, will aid you in every phase of the youngster's training.

Remember, never quit while you are losing – always quit when you are winning!! Once the atmosphere becomes relaxed, I repeat the exercise, each time applying a little more pressure to the nose and the riding crop until I receive a response from the horse to build on – even if it's one step back.

The main point to remember during this exercise is not to apply an excessive amount of pressure to the horse to instill injury or fear, which is very detrimental to the youngster's well being, as well as future training opportunities for the trainer.

The object of this exercise is to repeat it enough repetitious times, using the praise, repetition, patience training philosophy to teach the youngster to back up and begin the move-off-pressure learning phase until a desired effect is achieved.

A rule of thumb to remember is if too much pressure is applied, adverse conditions could develop including the horse bolting, rearing up and even flipping over backwards. It's important for the trainer to understand and realize the horse's body language at this juncture and know when enough is enough! A horse's body language will tell the trainer all he or she needs to know at this point.

As a legendary Hall of Fame Reined Cow Horse trainer once told me, " A bad trainer will make a great horse look bad but a great trainer will bring the best out in a horse and make the horse love its job – willingly."

Another important point to remember is when the youngster finally responds to the training and moves backwards, even if it's only one step, stop the pressure and praise the youngster. This exercise should be repeated daily until you can successfully back the youngster completely around the round pen in each direction – one full turn.

During negotiating this training exercise, the most important factor to remember is to discontinue the use of the riding crop training aid once your able to simply walk up to the youngster and back the horse completely around the round pen in each direction one full turn with light nose pressure and clucks. Once this accomplished your ready to move on to the next phase of training.

Step 2:

Since you're doing so well with your training, now let's bring the youngster to the next training phase: working the youngster without a halter and longe line in the round pen. To initiate this training phase, I walk the youngster to the center of the round pen, remove the longe line and halter, release the youngster and begin the longeing process. What I usually do is allow the youngster to meander around the round pen wall until it settles down and becomes accustomed to being in the round pen unrestrained. At this point the youngster should be accustomed to the popping sound of the longe whip training aid and longeing in the round pen.

This training phase incorporates every aspect of the youngster's training while on the longe line: walk, trot, canter, transitions and WHOA. This training exercise should be repeated daily until you can successfully negotiate these training requirements and bring your youngster from a walk to a trot to a lope and back down the scale i.e., canter, trot, walk, and WHOA with ease.

If for any reason any portion of this training exercise becomes problematic, please return to the longe line training apparatus until you can accomplish this training phase with ease and without problems or deficiencies in your program.

Step 3:

Once your youngster is negotiating the transitions and stopping with ease, the next phase of training involves the stop, back-up and roll back. I perform my warm-up in the usual manner and perform at least one full set of transitions in one direction only. Afterwards, I'll ask for the transitions until I reach a lope. Once at a lope, I'll ask for more speed from the youngster until a really fast gallop is achieved.

I then pick a spot in the round pen and step in the direction the youngster is heading at a 45-degree angle with the longe line extended. When I reach the head of the horse, I'll begin popping the longe whip in front of the horse until a sliding stop is achieved. At this point you should be in a position where the longe whip is blocking the forward motion of the horse. At this point I lay the longe whip on the front shoulder of the horse and begin tapping on the off or outside shoulder to begin the back up.

When the horse starts backing up, I encourage the youngster to turn into the round pen wall and roll over its hocks by moving its hip to the outside. After the horse learns to turn into the wall and turn in the opposite direction by rolling over its hocks, I move my position back and away from the horse and just let it walk or trot around the round pen until it settles.

The rule of thumb to remember is never to allow the youngster to develop a bad habit of turning away from the round pen wall and facing you. The horse should always turn into the round pen wall – never away! The object of this training is multi-faceted. First, you're gaining more control over the youngster, 2) the youngster is learning to use its hip to stop in a smooth and controlled manner, 3) this training allows the trainer to judge what kind of stop the horse will actually have in the show pen, 4) your developing a willing-partner bond between horse and trainer and 5) the youngster is learning to work on its own and unrestrained.

This training requires many hours in the round pen before the youngster becomes fluid, smooth and correct in this maneuver. I normally spend approximately 30 minutes a day on this training. The important items to remember for your horse is leg protection, bell boots and sliding boots. Never work without them!

Step 4:
This next phase of training involves preparing your horse for saddling. The first step I take is re-application of the no-

42

pull halter and hooking the youngster up in its stall. In preparation of the girth tightening, I accustom the horse to feeling pressure on its girth line with the aid of a lead rope.

I position the lead rope over the back of the youngster, reach under the horse and grab the lead rope with my off hand, all the while observing the horse. If the youngster is not too worried about the lead rope being over its body, I place the two pieces of the lead rope in one hand and gradually apply pressure to the horse's girth line by pulling up and holding the rope in one position until another position of pressure can be achieved.

If for some reason the horse resents this training phase, keep repeating it until you can simply place the rope over its back and take up the slack until a desired position of pressure is achieved. I normally increase the amount of time I hold the pressure until a desired effect is achieved. Repeat this exercise as often as required to accomplish the training goal.

A rule of thumb to remember is to teach your horse to girth-up in a gradual manner – one increase of pressure at a time. If improperly performed, this will develop an undesirable habit for the horse, which can quite possibly stay with the horse for the rest of its life and become problematic with each saddling and girthing session.

Step 5:

When the youngster becomes accustomed to this phase of training, I enlist the aid and introduction of my next training aid: a bareback pad. I use a bareback pad for two reasons: 1) it's light and 2) it has a girth strap.

I begin this next exercise while I have the youngster in the comfort of its stall with the no-pull halter attached. I let the youngster see the pad, realize it's not something to be afraid of, smell it and overall become accustomed to the sight of it. When desensitizing is accomplished, and the youngster becomes accustomed to me entering its stall with

43

the bareback pad, I begin the next phase of training and that's allowing the youngster to become accustomed to feeling the pad on its back, or more commonly referred to as "sacking out."

Once the youngster is accustomed to the pad being placed on its back and it is relaxed, I reach under the horse and begin the girthing process all over again by reaching under the horse, bringing the girth up and applying pressure with my hand only and without attaching it to the girth ring.

If at any point the horse becomes startled or exhibits signs of fear, I start over and repeat the process as often as necessary until a relaxed mood and atmosphere is achieved. After awhile the horse will become accustomed to the bareback pad and is ready for the next phase of training in the round pen.

Step 6:
The next phase of training involves bringing the youngster and the bareback pad to the round pen for longeing. I usually perform a pre-longeing preparation in advance of this training exercise. The longe line with the nose chain attached and the longe line are already pre-positioned in the round pen. I carry the bareback pad with me to the round pen while leading the youngster and once I arrive, I let the youngster observe me placing it on top of the round pen wall for desensitizing purposes.

I bring the youngster to the center of the round pen, hook it up to the longe line and begin performing a usual longe-line training exercise, which allows the youngster to warm up properly and observe the new object and addition hanging on top of the longe pen wall: the bare back pad.

Don't become alarmed if the youngster spooks at the bareback pad on the fence. This is just a phenomenon with horses. I've actually experienced a horse exhibit no signs of an object in one direction and then shy away from the same stationary object while passing in the opposite direction.

After the warm-up is complete, I retrieve the bareback pad and bring the youngster to the center of the round pen, position the pad on the youngster's back and girth to a desired level. The most important and critical point to remember during this training phase, is that the youngster may not want to move with the bareback pad girthed up and after encouragement by the trainer to move forward, the youngster may want to buck after taking the first couple of steps.

It's important for the trainer to visualize the body language and anticipate this pre-bucking posture: ears laid back, body in a locked-up position, tail swishing or tail flattened tightly against the horses butt. These are the telltale signs that a horse wants to crow hop or buck. The trainer should be ready for these two undesirable maneuvers and be prepared to stop it. If this is not corrected at this point, it will become even more problematic while performing the same training exercise when under saddle as the youngster grows older.

The important rule of thumb to remember is to warm your youngster up properly first and prior to saddling and hopefully this will diminish the opportunity of bucking. However, it's not a full-proof guarantee.

The final phase of training incorporates the horse being under saddle while performing the round-pen exercises. When the youngster can be successfully longed in the round pen on a longe line and without halter and longe line, it's time for the saddle.

To saddle the horse just return to the stall and repeat the steps performed during the bareback pad training and repeat until the horse can be safely saddled and stands relaxed in its stall.

Repeat the round-pen exercise in the exact manner as previously stated in the bareback pad segment.

When the horse can be saddled, longed properly in each direction while stopping, rolling back over his hocks and

45

leaving in the opposite direction, and performs the round - pen transitions - walk, trot, canter and WHOA with ease, the youngster will be ready for the first ride.

CHAPTER 4

2-YEAR-OLD COLT BREAKING 101
ART OF THE ROUND PEN
SADDLING, RIDING AND TRAINING

In the previous 2-Year-Old Colt Breaking chapter, I discussed the round-pen procedures for teaching the youngster to move off pressure, backing up, introduction of the riding crop training aid, round penning (with and without a halter), negotiating transitions (walk, jog, lope – on and off the longe line), as well as longeing with the bareback pad.

Peppys Angel Telesis and her weanling Dual N For Me

This chapter, which includes saddling, riding and training the 2-year-old, was developed using a ranch stallion Dual N For Me as a model and spans a documented time frame depicting the horse's life from the time he was born, being broke and started as a 2-year-old, as well as all training phases he completed at the ranch along the way to becoming a finished reined cow horse in all required disciplines: snaffle bit, bosal, two-rein, finished bridle horse and showing.

The main point to remember is that all horses I start and train are trained and started in the round pen in the exact same manner, no matter what performance horse discipline the youngster ultimately ends up performing in. This ensures a properly balanced horse and a training foundation that will last a lifetime and become the foundation and building block for future training. As a Quarter Horse breeder, I breed the "best" to the "best-available" and hope for the best but, as we all know, not every horse will ultimately perform in the desired discipline hoped for.

Dual N For Me as a 2-year-old, broke and started under saddle and in reining training with Rick in the saddle

The above photograph illustrates Dual N For Me being trained under saddle after successfully completing training in all phases in the round pen: walk, jog, lope transitions (with halter and longe line and without halter, bareback pad and under saddle) as well as backing up, stopping and turning into the round pen wall in the proper manner.

Step 1:

The next preparatory training phase involves flexing and bending on the ground for saddling, riding and training under saddle. This training phase begins by just being on the ground next to the youngster and using the nose chain to bend the youngster's head toward the left or right. At first, take what the youngster gives you. Once at the stopping point, release the youngster's head and bring it back again until a little more bend is accomplished. Keep repeating until a full bend and hold is accomplished.

One important factor to remember is: never tie a horse's head around and leave it tied around to struggle on its own while it is attempting to free itself. This is a very dangerous proposition and can, in some instances, ruin the youngster for future training opportunities, which can be spurned by resentment and fear or cause a serious injury.

When performing this training exercise, and for some reason the youngster begins to move on the ground, you're bending the horse's head too far, too quick and too soon.

Decrease the amount of bend and speed until the desired results are obtained.

When you're able to bend the horse's head around on the side you're mounting on, and you are able to hold onto the saddle horn without the horse fighting the maneuver, you're ready for the next training phase.

This next phase of training involves being in the saddle and riding the youngster. To prepare the horse for mounting and riding, I place the youngster in the stall fully saddled with a no-pull halter that has the lead rope attached to the ring at the bottom of the halter that is tied with a slip knot to the ring on the stall wall.

49

Dual N For Me as a 3-year-old, started on cattle, with cutting and cow horse training. Rick is in the saddle

Next, I begin a series of tests to determine how far the youngster is going to allow me to go in getting in the saddle. At first, I simply put my foot in the stirrup and apply a little weight pressure. If no objection is indicated by the horse, I increase the weight in the stirrup until I'm standing in the stirrup alongside the horse, all the while talking to the youngster in a calm and soothing voice.

When I'm able to stand up in the stirrup, I begin the process of swinging my leg completely over the horse and repeat daily until I'm able to completely get up in the saddle and swing my leg over the horse with ease, thus accomplishing saddle entry and simply sitting in the saddle astride the youngster.

When I'm able to just walk up to the horse and climb aboard, I enlist the aid of another individual or trainer to complete the remainder of the training process. I first put a regular halter over the no-pull halter and attach a lead rope with a nose chain, forming a double halter set up, with the assistant holding both lead ropes.

After I am in the saddle, the assistant asks for the youngster to walk around the perimeter of the stall. If a horse shows any warning signs of wanting to crow hop or buck, I immediately dismount and repeat the exercise until the helper can walk me completely around the stall in each direction without mishap. The most critical point in this training exercise is in the first one or two steps. Usually, if a horse is going to crow hop or buck, this is the time when the explosion occurs. When the horse can be mounted in the stall and led around with the rider aboard in each direction without incident, it's time to move to the next training phase.

Step 4:

The next phase of training begins in the round pen in the exact same manner as in the stall. The first item on the agenda is exercising the youngster in the round pen by going each direction prior to mounting and riding. After round penning, I bring the horse to the center of the arena and attach the no-pull halter and lead rope. Next, the horse is bridled with a headstall that has an O-ring snaffle bit, leather curb strap and reins attached. (For information only: all of my bits and spurs are made by Tom Balding and my headstalls and reins are all made by Custom Rawhide.)

The lead rope is then handed to the assistant. I pull the youngster's head around to the side I'm mounting from and step up and into the saddle with the horse's head still pulled around. For added security, I leave the horse's head tilted in this manner while the assistant steps the horse off in one direction or another.

Once the youngster walks around the round pen in each direction, making one turn each way without mishap, I ask the assistant to remove the lead rope and I'm off on my own. If for any reason the youngster stops and refuses to move, I enlist the aid of the English riding crop training aid and simply tap the horse's shoulder to promote movement. Before I start training, I allow the youngster to roam around the round pen at will until the horse becomes relaxed and accustomed to me being in the saddle while it's walking around. When I'm comfortable, I release the horse's head and allow the youngster to walk around the round pen following its nose.

Dual N For Me as a 3-year-old receiving his Reining Championship Circuit Award with Rick holding him.

Step 5:

When I start training in the round pen astride the youngster, I just start with what the horse gives me. Usually it's just a simple walk out and WHOA. Then I move to the walk, jog and back down to the walk and WHOA. The last portion of this training incorporates the lope and then back down to the jog, to the walk and WHOA.

If for any reason the youngster balks or refuses to execute these training maneuvers, except the WHOA, I incorporate and use the English riding crop as a means of propulsion for getting the youngster to move out.

A 4-year-old Dual N For M, shown cutting with Rick aboard riding two-handed.

Dual N For Me being worked one-handed in cutting competition by Rick.

One rule of thumb to remember is when teaching a youngster to WHOA and it won't respond, alternate pulling back on one rein or another to complete this action. Another rule of thumb to remember is never pull back on both reins at the same time as this action will be used in the next step to teach the horse to back up.

Dual N For Me as a 5-year-old being ridden by Rick's student Jolie Gasquet.

To illustrate what this round-pen training will evolve into when it's complete, refer to the above photograph of an actual training session with the stallion Dual N For Me with my student Joliet Gasquet in the saddle. The horse is performing all of the maneuvers it's required to perform, all the while being light and collected in a smooth, fluid and controlled manner.

Step 6:

The last training phases in the round pen relates to the backup, rollbacks, lead departures and spins. In order to accomplish the backup, pull back on both reins and ask for the backup. If the horse doesn't respond, release the pressure and ask for the backup again, while adding a little more pressure. If the youngster refuses to back up by locking its front legs, reach up and slap the youngster on one shoulder or the other but never with a spur or the heel of a boot but with the flat side of your foot. Keep practicing this maneuver until the youngster performs the backup smooth and collected.

When you reach this point, start the horse backing up and while backing up, pull the horse's head into the round pen wall while releasing pressure from the off-outside hand and applying pressure with the inside leg to move the horse's hip to the outside and use the outside leg and outside rein to push the horse through the rollback once the youngster has started to turn. The main point to remember is that once you've negotiated the rollback, take off at a brisk jog.

Once the youngster is proficient at the brisk jog departure, apply a little more pressure with the outside leg and ask for the departure at a lope. If the youngster doesn't respond at first, depart at a brisk jog and ask for the lope at a brisk long jog but make sure the youngster departs into a lope on the correct lead.

This training exercise is vital and important to teach the youngster to move its shoulders out of the way, especially when the colt or filly is destined for the cutting pen or working cattle.

When the youngster becomes proficient in the round pen when performing backups and rollbacks, the next training phase is adding the spins. To accomplish this training exercise, begin by backing the horse and rolling it over its hocks, but instead of going somewhere, just catch the horse once it has turned and continue the turnaround to the outside and use the round-pen wall as a buddy to help you complete one complete turnaround.

If the youngster balks, use the English riding crop to coax the youngster on by tapping on its outside shoulder or the shoulder away from the direction you're moving to complete the maneuver. Eventually the youngster will be moving off your leg, negotiating the turnaround or spin and learning to plant its back foot as a stabilizer.

When you complete this training and it has been performed correctly, you will have a willing partner that performs light and collected in a smooth, fluid and controlled manner. By the time you finish this training, the youngster is ready to move on to the last phase of training a cutting, reining and cow horse.

CHAPTER 5

2-YEAR-OLD COLT BREAKING 101
WARM UPS AND COLLECTION

In the last chapter, I discussed the colt's training in the round pen. If all of your training is going as planned, i.e., the colt can perform walk, jog and lope transitions, rollbacks, backups, spins and move off leg- and rein-pressure – right and left, it's time to move from the round pen training environment and to the main arena.

I use this same warm-up training exercise whether I'm preparing to show a cutting horse, reining horse or a cow horse. If the warm-up is properly performed, the horse becomes more supple, balanced, relaxed and a more proficient performer in the show pen.

Prior to performing this series of training exercises, it's important for the horse to be properly flexed, bent and collected at the poll. I use the following training exercise to collect a horse at the poll:

First, I simply alternate my hands to bump the colt's head down, with its chin perpendicular to the ground from a stand still.

Once the colt's head is at the desired configuration, I gather up a little more of the reins and ask the colt to back up. After a few steps, while still holding the colt's head in the desired position, I stop the colt and bump him into the bit by asking him to move forward. If the colt attempts to raise his head, I ask for the stop, bump the colt's head down (if required) and repeat the backup, thus repeating the exercise.

If the colt doesn't raise his head when moving forward, I release the pressure, which rewards the colt. I keep repeating this back-and-forth exercise until the colt's head is at the desired position and the colt is no longer resisting the training exercise and holds its head in the desired position with little or no coaxing. Ideally, the colt's nose should be perpendicular to the ground. If the colt's nose is forward of this position, he is "ahead of the bit". If the colt's nose is behind this position, he is "behind the bit." Both are undesirable positions.

Rick and Dualin Dude, 2005 AQHA sorrel gelding (Dualin Oak x Stella Peaches), NRHA/MSRHA Jr. Reining Champion and money earner. Note excellent head collection for left lead departure

To illustrate the ideal collection and framing of a horse, you can simulate this positioning by bending a riding crop with your hands located at each end. The riding crop should have a bow in the front end and a resulting bow in other end with a rise in the middle, simulating the horse's back.

A desired collection is necessary due to the fact that

most of a horse's power emanates from the hindquarters. A successful collection will allow the horse to travel more fluid, at ease, and with acceleration and stopping being achieved with greater fluidity. This is directly attributable to a proper collection and with the horse's hocks traveling underneath him. Before you attempt this next series of training exercises, the horse should collect well and travel in the proper position.

Rick and Dualin Oak, a 1999 AQHA chestnut stallion (Mister Dual Pep x Tessa Oak x Docs Oak) in collection training using the martingale and an O-Ring snaffle bit, demonstrating the desired collection position.

The beauty of the Vaquero training style is that a horse learns to perform in many different training disciplines over a specified period of time while using and being accustomed to performing in a variety of training apparatuses. Each training apparatus is designed to advance the colt's training and results in a very well-trained, smooth and fluid bridle horse.

Rick and Lil Red, a 4-year-old mare, transitioning from the O-Ring snaffle bit to the bosal, reinforcing collection training

Step 1:

In preparation of performing the next exercise, I saddle the colt, complete with all safety gear, and proceed to the round pen. Once at the round pen, I warm the horse up in the usual manner. Once the warm-up is complete, I climb aboard and put the colt through the normal training exercises listed above until I'm satisfied the colt is ready and relaxed to move to the next training environment: the main arena.

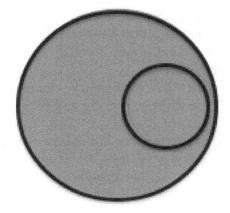

Once in the main arena, I walk the colt right or left, executing a very large circle making sure the colt is moving along relaxed while ensuring the colt is traveling inside his same tracks as in the above example:

When I have the desired size circle achieved, I tip the colt's nose to the inside of the circle in the direction I'm traveling and begin the training transitions: walk, jog and lope. The desired effect is to have the colt's nose tipped just a little to the inside of the circle I'm traveling so I can see his eye.

The other main focus is to have both reins touching the colt's neck and the colt traveling relaxed, framed up between the bridle reins with just a little bend to the inside of the direction I'm traveling and in a smooth, controlled and relaxed manner. It is very important in this stage of the colt's training for the rider to constantly remain in the center of the colt, without leaning to one side or the other, thus achieving the proper balance for horse and rider.

Once the colt is achieving the desired training in the large circle, I add a small circle to the inside of the large circle, see the above circle, to accustom the colt to the transition from a large circle to a small circle, which is the same maneuver used in a reining class. If you are loping, always ask the colt to slow down prior to entering the small circle. The inside hand is the direction hand and the outside hand is the speed-control hand. Once through the small circle, go back to the large circle.

Perform this exercise in proficiency increments beginning with the walk, next the jog or jog and finally the lope.

The main focal point to remember in the lope is not to allow the youngster to develop a habit of dropping the inside shoulder in the circle. If this becomes a problem, apply a little upward pressure with the inside hand to encourage the colt to hold his shoulder up. If the youngster yaws to the outside of the circle, apply a little leg pressure to hold his ribs in and hold him in place. Once I'm able to successfully achieve all of the maneuvers in each direction, then - and only then - do I add a little more training to the youngster's training regimen.

Step 2:

The next training exercise I perform is stopping the colt, initiating the backup and backing the colt around the circle once each way. Once the colt is proficient in backing around the circle, I add the next training phase: backing the colt up and rolling him over his hocks to successfully complete a rollback. As is done in the round pen, it's important for the colt to go somewhere immediately following the rollback. This will accustom the colt to use his hindquarters to propel himself out of the maneuver once it's successfully completed.

If you're traveling to the left, roll back to the right. If you're traveling to the right, roll back to the left, always ensuring the colt's hip is moved out of the way. This will simulate the training you should have already instilled in the colt in the round pen. The only difference is the absence of the round-pen wall. This training will help the colt gain confidence by completing maneuvers outside the round pen in an open area and absent of the round-pen wall.

Once the colt is proficient jogging out of the maneuver at a brisk pace, then - and only then - ask the colt for a lead departure once through the rollback. Simply pick the rein up in the direction your headed, push the colt out of the rollback with your leg and depart into a smooth and controlled lope. Once the correct lead departure is negotiated, sit back, relax and enjoy the ride. The main point to remember at this juncture in the colt's training is to ensure the colt remains focused, framed up, collected, relaxed and executes the maneuvers in a smooth, controlled and fluid manner.

It's also important to ask for the transitions in all phases of training, e.g., walk, jog, lope and lope, jog, walk. Never ask for a complete stop from a lope in the circle because this can develop undesirable training and performance issues later on when training the colt for high-speed stops or when working cattle.

Another important aspect of this training to remember is never attempt a lead departure from a standstill. Instead, walk off about three steps with the colt's head and body in the proper collection and frame position, with his nose tipped in the proper direction, and ask for the lead departure. This will allow for a more fluid lead departure into a lope. The first photo of this article is a very good illustration of a correct lead departure in an NRHA reining class with me riding a 3-year-old Dualin Oak colt .

Step 3:
Once this training exercise can successfully be completed, it's time to add a little more training by adding an additional circle, thus completing a Figure 8.

To accomplish this exercise, move to the out side of the circle and track another circle the same diameter along side the first circle to intersect and form a Figure 8. Now that you have the Figure 8 complete, the next step is to add two small circles to the inside of each large circle. From here, there are a lot of training exercises that can be completed using the Figure 8. I developed this training technique to train students, especially those students entering either the reining or cow-horse arenas.

To begin the exercise, I walk the colt to the center of the intersecting circles, stop the colt and begin the exercise – either right or left. Each time I reach the desired direction, I tip the colt's nose to the inside and apply a little inside leg pressure to let the colt know which direction we are going. Once in the desired direction, I focus on maintaining the colt in proper training mode until I reach the intersected circle. Prior to arriving at the intersection, I ask the colt to slow down using my outside rein while holding the inside or direction hand in the proper position.

Once in the intersection, I apply leg pressure with both legs to straighten or frame the colt up, execute the transition – if from a jog or lope – and prepare for the departure in the opposite direction. Once proficient at walking the Figure 8 with the colt, I then add the jog . Once proficient at the jog, I then add the lope.

The important aspect of the lope departure is to remember to walk the horse forward a few steps prior to asking for the lead departure instead of asking for a lead departure from a stand still. Another important aspect of executing these training exercises is to focus on maintaining the proper head collection and body framing at all times.

Once the lope is achieved, I again ask the colt to slow down to a jog or jog once in the intersection and prior to reaching the middle section of the intersecting circles, then go down to a walk if I'm planning to stop in the middle of the intersection. With each entry into the intersection, I straighten (frame) the colt up and prepare him for the next direction change with a transition, except at the walk. This training also sets the colt up for performing flying lead changes if this type of maneuver is desired in the next phase of training.

I'm constantly asked how much pressure I exert on a horse's mouth while training. My answer is simple. My desired amount of pressure exerted is approximately one-half an ounce, regardless of what training apparatus I'm using. I only use enough pressure to reach the desired training effect but I always strive to work my horses with as little pressure as possible to execute the maneuver.

One rule of thumb to remember is that once a colt learns and is proficient at flying lead changes, I never perform flying lead changes in the Figure 8 training exercise. This causes the colt to anticipate the lead change each time it comes to the middle of the Figure 8 and that will hurt you in the show pen.

Once the colt is proficient in the Figure 8, I alternate his training regimen by stopping and performing roll backs in the middle of the intersection or one and a half spins – right or left – to change directions and departures or stopping and moving forward to change directions. It's important to keep the horse off balance, which will deter the colt in anticipating a maneuver that is derived from too much repetition of one particular maneuver. Keeping the colt off balance will ensure he is listening to your direction and will deter him from anticipating a maneuver he thinks you're going to want to do.

Horses are very smart and learn quickly. As one Hall of Fame Reined Cow Horse trainer once told me, "It may take many times to teach a horse a particular maneuver but only one time to teach him a bad one!"

A typical training exercise performed by me in the Figure 8 training circles can consist of the following:

• I begin by walking the colt to the center of the intersecting circles. I complete one full set of circles by traveling in a large circle, into a small circle and return to the center, frame my horse up, travel to the opposite end of the circles, give simultaneous leg and hand cues in the direction I'm heading and travel off in the opposite direction while completing a large and small circle and returning to the middle of the Figure 8.

• Once at the center, I either stop and complete one-and-one-half spins – right or left – and travel off into the opposite direction while negotiating a large and small circle each way, or

• I stop in the middle, negotiate a rollback opposite of the direction I just performed and move off in the opposite direction while completing a full set of large and small circles each way and returning to the middle of the intersection.

This training exercise will produce a horse that is responsive, supple, willing and smooth with no resistance, if properly executed, as well as adding more control on the colt.

Katrina and Dualin Dude demonstrating the versatility of the American Quarter Horse, the properly trained reined cow horse and Wind River Ranch stock, Rick Dennis, trainer, Southern Eventing & Dressage.

Rick Dennis demonstrating how his stallion Dualin Oak can be shown in collected, performing dressage movements.

67

CHAPTER 6

ADVANCED TRAINING
CROSS TRAINING 101, HIGH-SPEED RUN DOWNS AND STOPS

This chapter is an advanced training course that is required in a Reined Cow Horse rein-work class and addresses one of the most intimidating portions of horsemanship that the beginning rider has to learn, cope and master, especially in the cutting, reining and cow horse pens: high-speed stops.

One of the biggest fears the beginner has to overcome is the fear of flying over the head of the horse and landing on this or her back while negotiating this maneuver. This is certainly a possibility if the rider is not 1) sitting in the middle of the horse's back, well balanced and relaxed, 2) prepared for the stop and 3) properly schooled in the execution of the maneuver prior to the happening.

The only way to overcome this fear of flying is to execute the maneuver over and over until the fear is faced and eliminated. This is usually accomplished by proficiency at a walk, next a jog and finally a lope while learning to successfully negotiate the maneuver, build speed and prepare for the stop along the way.

Before attempting this next phase of training, your horse should be able to stop with voice and bit pressure, collect, frame up and move off the leg and rein pressure right and left. If you're training your horse according to the instructions in training segments 1 through 5 then you and your horse should be prepared for this next training phase.

Prior to beginning this training phase, it's time to add another important aspect of the horse's stop in addition to the use of voice and hand control. This next step involves

68

walking the horse until the desired stopping location is identified and asking the horse to stop but each time you stop by using voice and reins, open your legs and throw them forward, toes up, heels down and brace your legs as if preparing for a high-speed stop.

Rick schooling Dualin Oak, a 1999 AQHA chestnut stallion (Mister Dual Pep x Tessa Oak x Docs Oak) in high-speed run downs and stops prior to a Junior Reining class.

The important phase of this training maneuver is decreasing the amount of voice and hand cues you give the horse until you reach a point where the horse stops when you simply open your legs and throw them forward. This is the same cue you will later use to stop the horse at a high rate of speed. Keep repeating this exercise until you and your horse are proficient using the leg cues. **Do not attempt the next maneuver until this action is accomplished!**

The object is to stop your horse in the show pen with as little hand movement as possible, which is more appealing to the judges and typically results in a more fluid stop and a higher score.

Another important training aid to teach your horse is for the horse to learn to depart and build up speed when the rider simply squeezes the sides of the horse with his or her calves instead of kicking the horse with the heel of the boot or with spurs – except when performing a lead departure, which requires the use of the leg opposite of the departure direction for propulsion which is achieved by gentle heel or spur taps or a gentle push. Slapping a horse with your leg in a reining class most often startles the horse and has an undesirable effect.

Step 1:

To prepare the horse and rider for this maneuver, the rider should locate the center of the arena length ways and either set a cone on the ground or tie a ribbon on the fence to indicate a starting point. Next, the rider should locate the center of the arena on the opposite end of the arena and either set a cone on the ground or tie a ribbon on the fence that should indicate a straight line from one end of the arena or the other. These two markers are your starting and ending points.

Step 2:

The horse and rider should take up a position in front of the beginning marker, which should align the equestrian team in line with the ending marker, creating an imaginary straight line.

When in position, the rider should have the horse framed up or the horse's head in-line with its hindquarters and in collection. To accustom the horse to traveling in a straight line, ask the horse to walk off with a gentle squeeze of your calves, headed toward the opposite end of the arena, all the while making sure the horse remains collected and framed up. Maintaining a framed position requires the rider to maintain equal leg pressure on each side of the horse to control the rib movement of the horse. If for any reason the horse becomes uncollected, stop the horse, back up a few steps, recollect the head and continue the maneuver.

If the horse tries to "yaw" or move out of position, right or left, apply leg pressure with the leg in the direction the horse is trying to move in and move the horse's ribs back in place to re-frame the horse. After the correction, the rider's legs should be draped on each side of the horse – down, relaxed and with the legs laid against or touching the horse. The rider should only use enough leg pressure to get the horse to respond to the correction and re-frame.

Once you arrive at the opposite end of the arena, allow the horse to walk toward the fence and let the fence stop the horse naturally. This will teach the horse the fence is a natural barrier it needs to respect and stop at upon arrival. The natural effect to overcome is teaching the horse to allow the fence to stop it in a straight line instead of the horse traveling right or left once reaching the barrier, which is a natural happening for the horse.

If this starts to become a problem, stop the horse in the direction it's trying to go in and turn it completely around in a spin in the opposite direction and reposition the horse

71

in a straight line facing the end barrier. This will teach the horse to stop straight, smooth, framed and collected. After the stop, sit there and praise your horse for about two or three minutes and let the horse relax. This will reward the horse after the maneuver and should be repeated after each stop.

A basic rule to remember is to never drive a horse into a fence, which could cause injury to the horse and rider. Use the fence as a buddy to initial phases. This should be completed successfully at a walk before adding the jog to the training regimen.

Chelsi Guillory and Some Hot Chic practicing in-line run downs.

The main points for the rider to remember are: 1) remain in position in the middle of the horse without leaning from side to side which provides unequal pressure for the horse,

2) practice your equitation: elbows against the body, hands forward an equal distance apart or shoulder width, back straight, body squared and chin slightly tucked and 3) **never lean backwards in the stop!**

The photo on the previous page illustrates horse and rider in perfect form while practicing the in-line run down and stop maneuver. The horse is in collection and framed up. The rider is in good equitation form, balanced and relaxed.

A better explanation of this style is illustrated by the definition of equitation. Equitation is "the art or practice of horse riding or horsemanship." More specifically, equitation may refer to a rider's position while mounted and encompass a rider's ability to ride correctly and with effective aids. Equitation classes occur in the hunt seat, saddle seat, dressage, and Western disciplines.

A good equitation rider is always in balance with the horse, maintains a correct position in every gait, movement, and possesses a commanding but relaxed presence, able to direct the horse with nearly invisible aids. Stopping the horse with the minimal amount of pressure and hand movement is good. Stopping the horse with leg cues only is optimal. Learn to ride your horse in this fashion and it will greatly help you in the show pen.

The video link (https://youtu.be/1h3b9ZtRcI4) of a student, Joliet Gasquet and her 3-year-old Quarter Horse mare Lil Red, fully illustrates the horse and rider learning to maneuver her horse by performing in-line lead departures which is the next maneuver following high-speed run downs and stops. This is the first step in teaching the horse in-line lead changes which eventually develop into flying lead changes. The principle of both maneuvers is the same: traveling in a straight line relaxed, collected and framed up.

Step 3:

Once the horse and rider are proficient at walking down the center of the arena in a straight line – collected, framed up, relaxed and allowing the horse to stop correctly – it's time to add a little more speed into the maneuver at a jog.

Once the rider is in position facing the opposite end of the arena, simply squeeze the horse off into a walk, add a little more leg pressure and ask the horse to jog, ensuring the horse remains framed-up and collected, especially at the departure and through the gate transition.

Prior to reaching the end of the arena, the rider should locate a predetermined location to stop the horse prior to arriving at the fence. The simple philosophy is allowing the horse to think he or she is going to the fence to stop and using this psychology to the rider's advantage in stopping the horse.

If the horse walks out of the stop or doesn't stop when asked, back the horse up after each stop until this action is corrected, being careful not to repeat the reinforcement more than necessary or you may instill an undesirable trait in the horse or the horse may back up without a request from the rider.

This exercise at a jog should be repeated as often as necessary until the horse and rider are proficient at the jog. One action the rider should begin to notice is the faster the jog the more often the horse is going to begin to drop its hip in the ground to complete the stop. I usually stay in the jog until I can complete the training exercise at an extended jog.

The last phase is completing the exercise at a lope. I generally start the horse off at a low speed lope and only increase speed as the horse becomes proficient at each speed increment. The rule to remember is if you can't control your horse at a slow speed, you can't control your horse at a faster speed. You should only increase speed after you and your horse become proficient at one particular speed.

If for any reason during the lope the horse begins to move its head up and out of collection, it's the responsibility of the rider to bump the horse's head down, even during the stop. This will allow the horse to stop framed and collected, which will allow for a smoother and longer stop.

Rick & Dual Train, a 1995 AQHA sorrel mare (Dual Peppy x Nics Train x Reminic) performing a high-speed run down and stop during the Rein Work at the NRCHA Derby, Medford, Oregon.

Ensure you are very proficient and comfortable in doing this training exercise prior to trying to perform it at a higher rate of speed. Holding on to the horn and trying to correct and stop the horse is strictly taboo and will only cause more problems for the horse and rider by positioning the equestrian team out of balance.

The primary objective for the horse to remain framed in a reining stop is for the horse to use its body positioning and weight (simple physics) to lengthen the slide. It's easier for a rider to do an eloquent rollback from this position than any other position. Another important factor to remember is to stop the horse well before the fence for safety purposes for both horse and rider. A horse's hindquarters are like air breaks on a truck; use them to your advantage.

Long stops that look like railroad tracks are accomplished by a high rate of speed. If you're not ready for it, don't do it. Stay in your comfort zone until you and your horse are ready for change. The more you practice and the faster the travel, the longer the stops.

Keep your hands and reins relaxed and next to the saddle horn for use if the need arises and stay out of the horse's mouth with the bit unless it's necessary.

At some point your horse will more than likely want to take control of the situation and gather speed at his or her own pace to please the rider, which is an undesirable trait. When this happens, stop the horse, back it up and continue the exercise until the horse learns it has to travel at the rider's directed speed and request. Stop and repeat until the undesirable action is corrected and the horse is building speed at the rider's direction.

The optimum action is for the horse and rider to build speed gradually and stop the horse at the height of the speed building. A horse running wide open and out of control down the center of the arena is undesirable for the horse and rider as well as the judges. It doesn't matter if your performance horse is in a reining, cutting or reined cow horse class, high-speed stops are part of the game and the exhibitor should become proficient and comfortable in the maneuver.

CHAPTER 7

ADVANCED TRAINING
EXECUTING AND MASTERING THE
TURNAROUND OR "SPIN"

Rick Dennis and Dual N For Me spinning left in a 3-Year-Old Junior Reining class.

At this point in your training, and if you've been training in line with the preceding training segments, you and your horse should negotiate the following round-pen maneuvers with ease.

Walk, jog, canter and stop in each direction, perform backups and rollbacks on the wall with ease as well as moving the colt's shoulders and front end out of the way with each rollback and direction change. The colt should also move off of direct rein and leg pressure.

The mechanics involved in turning a horse around is not an arduous affair and is actually quite simple. A turnaround is merely a forward movement in place. The two main points to remember is to use more leg pressure than rein pressure. One of the hardest portions of the turnaround (spin) is learning to move the horse's shoulders and frontend over while using more leg pressure to negotiate the maneuver than rein pressure. This is accomplished by laying the rein on the horse's neck as a direction cue (only) and applying enough leg pressure to initiate and complete the maneuver. I can't emphasize this enough – **"It's all leg pressure and not, rein pressure!"**

Effectively what happens when more rein pressure than leg pressure is applied is that your rein hand becomes positioned across the colt's neck and tips the horse's nose to the outside of the direction your attempting to turnaround (spin) in and binds the horse up. This "binding up" prevents the horse from negotiating a fluid, smooth and correct turnaround (spin).

The photograph on the previous page of me exhibiting Dual N For Me in a Junior Reining Class illustrates me turning the horse around (spinning) to the left and my right hand is simply cuing the horse to move off of rein pressure and to the left while my right leg is applying steady pressure to move the horse's shoulders and front end to the left to negotiate the complete turnaround (spin) on a stationary pivot foot.

To train the horse to turnaround (spin), begin at a walk in the round pen in either a right or left direction. After a few turns in the round pen, stop the horse, initiate a rollback into the opposite direction into the round pen wall.

Once you've completely made the turn into the opposite direction, stop the horse before the colt can walk off. Apply rein and leg pressure from the inside position, or position next to the round pen wall, while holding a little back pressure with the outside rein hand to prevent the colt from walking out of the maneuver. By using a series of gentle bumps, the outside hand can also be used to cue the colt in the desired direction.

Begin with quarter-turn increments. Once you've completely turned the colt around 360 degrees, stop the maneuver. At the conclusion, walk the horse off for a few complete turns around the round pen, stop the horse when you're ready and complete the maneuver in the opposite direction. The main point to remember is to use enough rein hand and leg pressure to give a direction cue and enough back pressure with the opposite rein hand to prevent the horse from conducting any forward movement to walk out of the maneuver.

If the colt balks or refuses to execute the maneuver, apply steady leg pressure and bump the colt's nose with the off hand into the desired direction and repeat as necessary to execute the maneuver. With enough practice and with correct hand and leg cues, the colt will catch on really fast and will surprise you at the speed the colt will begin negotiating the maneuver. Once the colt can perform this maneuver in quarter turns, expand the exercise to half turns and then a complete 360-degree turn.

In the end you should be able to complete the rollback, apply leg and rein pressure and complete the turnaround (spin) exercise in a fluid, controlled and disciplined manner.

Training Tips:
• **ONLY** use enough leg and rein cue pressure to successfully negotiate the training exercise.

• **NEVER** allow your direction hand to cross the neck of the horse, which will effectively pull the colt's nose to the outside and away from the turn around (spin) direction.

• **NEVER** stick the colt with a spur to cause injury, bleeding, or pain, which will cause a fear factor with the colt and will eventually develop into the colt fighting or refusing to negotiate the training exercise. Leg and spur pressure should be applied equally until enough pressure results in the colt moving off into the desired direction.

• **DO NOT** over execute this maneuver or the colt will eventually develop a bad habit of trying to anticipate the maneuver each time you practice a rollback. Once the maneuver is an accomplished training exercise in the round pen, only use this maneuver when necessary.

• Refrain from bitting the horse up with a more powerful bit, which will only cause problems. Keep with the same training bit the horse is accustomed to or the O-Ring snaffle.

• **NEVER** back a horse up and into a spin which will cause the horse to start bringing its outside leg underneath the inside leg and cause the horse to be choppy, or in the worse case scenario, balk in the maneuver.
•
• Fine tuning the spin from the round pen to the open arena:

Step 1:

The next phase of training involves walking out in the open arena and performing the box exercise. Basically, this maneuver involves walking the horse in a straight line and at a desired point turning the colt sharply – to the left or right - while applying equal leg and rein pressure to move the colt's shoulders and front end over and out of the way at the same time to change the direction.

Once the first corner of the box is complete, walk the colt in a straight line framed up until you reach another desired location and make another sharp turn in the same direction and repeat the leg and rein pressure until all four corners of the box are negotiated. The next step is to complete the box maneuver in the opposite direction.

Step 2:

Once the horse is fluid at performing the box maneuver, the next phase is teaching the colt to move off of leg and rein pressure in a small circle. To begin the exercise, tip the colt's nose in a right or left direction and walk the horse in a small circle, all the while closing the circle tighter with leg- and rein-pressure cues until the colt's nose can be tipped even more to the inside while applying back pressure with the off hand to stop forward motion. Leg pressure can be applied to turn the colt in a complete 360-degree turn-around (spin). At this juncture in the exercise, the colt's small circle should be tight enough to make you think he's about to stop from the tightness of the circle.

Once the spin is negotiated, DO NOT stop your horse but walk out of the spin and into a larger circle and in the same direction. Repeat this exercise for two or three more times and then change directions and repeat in the opposite direction. The main point to remember is to hold enough back pressure for the horse to develop the habit of working off one stationery pivot foot while negotiating the turnaround (spin). Another important main point is to never allow the horse to come out of collection. If this happens, bump the colt's head back into collection before completing the maneuver.

Step 3:

Cleaning up the turnaround (spin) requires the use of another very effective training exercise or the "counter canter" or "counter arc" as some refer to it. This basically requires walking the horse in a straight line and at some point tipping the colt's nose right or left and then applying a rein direction cue and enough leg pressure to move the colt off in the opposite direction. The main point to remember here is to always keep the colt moving forward and over. This motion will cause the colt to move its outside leg out and over the inside leg which will eventually allow the colt to perform a turnaround (spin) with lighting speed and still be very fluid. To end the exercise, turn the colt's head over, around and in the direction you are moving, much like performing a flex-and-bend exercise. After a few seconds, allow the colt to straighten up, travel in a straight line and framed up in order to complete the training maneuver in the opposite direction. Another main point to remember is if the colt at any point attempts to back out of the maneuver, straighten the colt up, move him forward and start the maneuver all over again.

The main focus of the exercise is to have your colt turning around in place on the pivot foot and with the outside leg crossing over the inside leg. To check yourself, look on the ground after the maneuver and see if there is a perfect hole in the ground made by the pivot foot and encompassing this circle is a perfect box that is made by the colt's front leg during the maneuver.

Rick and Dual N For Me, 3-Year-Old Junior Reining Champions.

CHAPTER 8

ADVANCED TRAINING
EXECUTING AND MASTERING LEAD CHANGES

Rick and Dualin Dude, the 4-year-old Reining Champions and money earners at the MSRHA/NRHA Reining in Forrest, Miss.

At this point in your training and if you've been training inline with the preceding training segments, you and your horse should negotiate the following round-pen maneuvers with ease: Walk, jog, lope and stop in each direction, Back ups and rollbacks on the wall with ease and Move the colt's shoulders and front end out of the way with each rollback and direction change.

The most important lesson to learn from these training segments is: "There is no substitute for learning proper horsemanship," in an equine training environment. Therefore, the next phase of training is to build on the success of the above training exercises and learn to control the colt's body from the tip of its nose to its hindquarters as well as all locations in between.

Before attempting this training segment, the colt should have been on a progressive training schedule with each successful phase of training being the building platform for the next one. In this article, it's the lead departure and the lead change that some students find very hard to learn and almost impossible to execute. However, the correct and effective lead change can be a very rewarding experience once the training exercise is learned and the execution is properly performed.

Step 1:
Disengaging the front shoulders and hindquarters

Begin the next training exercise by facing the wall of the round pen and decide whether you want to move the horse's hindquarters to the left or right. For this lesson, let's decide to move the horse's hindquarters to the right. To accomplish this maneuver, pick up the right rein and lay it on the right neck of the horse while using the off hand and rein to keep the shoulders in place and prevent any movement to the right when the hindquarters are disengaged and moved.

To move the colt's hindquarters to the right, simply put your left leg toward the rear of the horse's rib cage, but not in the flank area, and apply leg pressure to disengage the hindquarters and move them to the right. Be careful not to let the horse's front end, move in unison with the hindquarters. Once the hindquarters are disengaged and moved out of the way, move your left leg to the left girth area, apply enough leg pressure and left neck-rein pressure to move the colt's front end to meet the hindquarters.

Complete this training exercise in three repetition stages

84

and then walk off and make a few turns around the round pen in the same direction you just moved the horse in to allow the colt to relax. The main point to remember is only use enough leg and spur pressure to move the colt's front end over and disengage the hindquarters to move them in the desired direction, with the direction being determined at the discretion of the rider.

If you use too much pressure, you could hurt the colt or make the training exercise unpleasant. The colt will stiffen up and the maneuver will become more and more difficult to perform. The object is to gain complete control of your horse's body movements with hand and leg cues that will allow a controlled, fluid and correct movement later on both the lead departure and the lead change.

Once the horse is fully relaxed, face the round-pen wall and execute the training exercise in the opposite direction or in this case to the left. The main point to remember is to gradually increase the amount of training exercise routines until the colt's body can be moved in each direction with ease by applying the correct leg pressure and rein cues. If the colt makes a big fuss over the exercise, just get the horse to perform one, then relax the colt and execute another one and so on.

Another point to remember is to gradually decrease the amount of leg pressure with the spur over time until the maneuver can be accomplished with light calf and foot pressure (only). Bear in mind that once you and your horse become proficient in this training exercise, teaching the horse to side pass would be the next logical step in training. Eventually, the rider should be able to disengage the colt's hindquarters and move the colt in a 360-degree circle by disengaging and moving its hindquarters.

Step 2:
Performing Figure 8s At An Extended Long Jog

Once you're able to move the colt's body with subtle leg

85

and hand cues, including moving the ribs in and out on each side, I like to reinforce my hand and leg cues by performing figure 8s in an open arena at an extended long jog. In order to complete this training exercise, move to the middle of the arena, pick a direction and move off at a walk while maintaining a proper head collection, with the colt's body framed up, and perform a complete figure 8. The initial direction should be determined at the rider's discretion. Once accomplished, hold a little back pressure to maintain a proper head collection while using both legs simultaneously to apply proper leg pressure to encourage a forward propulsion and proper speed to enter an extended long jog, without the colt's headset coming out of collection.

While in the extended long jog, negotiate the figure 8 using proper rein-hand and leg placement to maintain a complete circle until you reach the diagonal or center of the arena entry point. Upon entering the diagonal, slow the colt down and use proper rein-hand position on both sides of the colt's neck while simultaneously applying leg pressure with both legs to move the colt's ribs in, effectively framing the horse up while coming through the diagonal. Once you are through the diagonal, resume the correct speed to regain the extended long jog. This framed-up position and speed transition through the diagonal will be used later to negotiate a successful lead change. So practice for proficiency and with as light a cue pressure as possible. Maintaining a proper head collection is essential to a successful maneuver.

Step 3:
Performing High-Speed Figure 8 Lead Changes
When I have the colt proficient in the figure 8, I simply walk off, negotiate a lead departure, either on a right or left lead, and begin building speed with each complete turn in the circle. At this point, if you're on a right lead, most of

86

your weight should be on the inside legs of the colt (the legs in the inside of the circle), leaving the outside legs with less weight.

Your horse's nose should be tipped to the inside and your inside leg should be applying a little pressure as a direction and bending of the rib cage cue, with your outside leg laid on the colt to keep the horse from drifting out of the circle. If you've ever watched a group of horses playing in a pasture, they execute lead changes at will with each direction change, which is a natural movement for the horse.

In order to capitalize and build on this natural movement, I simply have the horse moving as fast as possible in the right circle, without a speed transition in the diagonal. Before reaching the end of the diagonal, I shift my weight to the left, tip the horse's nose to the left, release my inside or left-leg pressure and apply outside or right-rein and leg pressure while turning the colt in the opposite direction, or to the left, to produce a natural lead change transition.

If for some reason the colt misses the lead change, just allow the horse to travel around the circle on the wrong lead for a few turns and then slow the horse down, execute the lead change to the left and continue through a 360-degree circle while traveling and building speed all the time.

When you're ready to execute the lead change to the right, just repeat the process. Eventually, and with enough practice, the colt will learn these high-speed, flying lead changes with the aid of proper weight distribution, hand and leg cues and the proper pressure. At the conclusion, you should be able to complete a 360-degree circle, come through the diagonal, frame up and swap directions on the proper lead change and complete the figure 8. The main point to remember in this exercise is not to become frustrated when and if the colt misses a lead change.

87

Simply make the proper correction until you and the colt become proficient in the maneuver and the colt learns what you're asking him to do.

Step 4 – Inline Lead Departures and Lead Changes

To clean up the lead departure and the lead change, I next incorporate inline lead departures and lead changes in a straight line. I like to conduct this training exercise on a racetrack or in a long field if the arena I'm working in isn't long enough. If you choose to use the latter method, make sure the field is mowed properly and walk the field to make sure it doesn't contain any holes, obstacles or trash that could cause an injury or harm to you and your horse. The main point to remember is that you're working on grass and use precaution to prevent slipping during the maneuver.

I start this training exercise by walking the colt forward a few steps, pick up the desired direction hand as a cue by moving the colt's jaw, move the horses hip and front shoulder in the direction I want to depart in and lope off in the correct lead. After I'm in the desired lead departure and traveling in a straight line, I frame the colt up and make sure proper head collection is incorporated in the maneuver before attempting the next phase of training, which is stopping the colt and repeating the entire exercise to depart on the opposite lead. I usually allow the colt about 15 to 20 full strides before I stop him to negotiate the next maneuver, which allows the horse to relax.

When I'm ready, I stop the colt, allow the horse to further relax and repeat the exercise on the opposite lead. Always allow the colt to relax and think about what's happening before you initiate the maneuver again. I'll execute this maneuver in repetition until I reach the end of the arena, the field or my starting point if I'm working on a racetrack. The main point to remember with this training exercise is that you're working on a lot of maneuvers in one exercise: lead departures, framing the colt, disengaging the hindquarters, head collection, leg cues, rein cues, stops and traveling in a straight line.

When and only when I have the colt performing this training exercise with ease, do I move onto the next phase: performing simple inline lead changes. The main point to remember is to not exhaust your colt during this training exercise. I've found a good starting point is to perform three or four stops and starts in each direction and build endurance accordingly.

Step 5 – Simple Lead Changes

This next phase of training is quite simple if Step No. 4 is an accomplished training exercise executed by horse and rider. To begin the exercise, begin at a starting point, walk the colt off, execute a lead departure in your direction of choice, frame the colt up and after 15 or 20 full strides, break the colt down to a jog instead of a stop, all the while keeping the horse properly framed and properly collected. While jogging a few times, pick up the rein and cue the colt in the lead you wish to pick up by moving its nose in that direction, just as if you were executing a lead departure.

Next release the leg pressure in the direction on the lead you wish to change to and use the opposite leg to apply pressure to facilitate the lead change. This is not a hard exercise to execute! All that's happening is that you're executing a lead departure from a jog instead of a walk; however, this will accustom the colt to listening to your hand and leg cues and will prepare the colt for the next phase of training – the flying lead change. After about 15 to 20 full strides, break the colt down to a jog and repeat the training exercise for the opposite lead change.

A few main points to remember are to keep the colt traveling in a straight line at all times, framed up and with a proper head collection. If for any reason this can't be accomplished, return to stopping and starting the colt until the situation can be remedied. Another main point to remember is to become proficient in one phase before moving on to another phase of training.

Step 6 – Flying Lead Changes

To execute this maneuver of flying lead changes, I decrease the amount of jogs I allow the colt to make before I move through the diagonal, pick up the colt's nose in the direction I want to change to and ask for the lead change while at a jog. A main point to remember is not to wear your horse out in practice. A tired horse will be non-responsive and tough to deal with. Always practice on a well-conditioned and fresh horse. The training will wear the colt out soon enough!

I only ask for the flying lead change after I can proficiently negotiate a lead change from one jog only. To accomplish this, I break the horse to one jog and immediately make the proper rein-hand and leg cues to execute the proper lead change. Remember, if the colt misses the lead change, don't panic or become frustrated. Simply stop the colt and start the entire process over but in the direction he missed the lead change. This will teach him he missed the proper execution.

When the colt is proficient in the one jog pick up, I eliminate the jog, make the exact hand and leg cues and ask for the lead change at a lope. What works best for me is disengaging the hindquarters first and immediately moving my leg forward to move the front end over and into the proper lead. If for some reason the colt refuses to give you the flying lead change, break the colt down to a stop and repeat the entire walk-jog-lope lead change process until the colt performs a flying lead change on request with sufficient rein-hand and leg pressure cues.

To eliminate the possibility of the colt anticipating the lead change while executing the figure 8 training regimen, I only practice the flying lead change maneuver in the inline training exercise. I perform more figure 8s at an extended long jog and save the lead change on the diagonal right before a show. The extended long jog will provide you with a training exercise that is actually better for getting the colt in working condition than any other exercise you may use to leg your horse up and maintain him or her in top physical condition.

As with all training, proficiency comes with proper understanding, horsemanship training, execution, practice, repetition and commitment. With the proper training, the lead departure and lead change can be accomplished in a relatively short period of time by any committed equestrian enthusiast.

CHAPTER 9

ADVANCED TRAINING
STARTING YOUNG HORSES ON CATTLE
FROM A MULTI-EVENT TRAINER'S
VIEWPOINT

Rick Dennis working two handed on Dual Train, competing in a reined cow horse herd-work class.

After answering a myriad of questions pertaining to my young horses on cattle, this chapter addresses this complex issue from my professional multiple-event trainer's point of view, addressing both cutting horses and reined cow horses.

First and foremost, a cow horse is a cow horse whether it's a cutting horse or a reined cow horse. Both have to work cattle in the cutting pen. The difference between the two is a cutting horse is trained to work a parallel line with the cow while the reined cow horse is taught to step to and chase the cow, except when the reined cow horse is performing herd work in a reined cow horse class. Then the horse also has to work a parallel line but is assisted and handled by the rider.

Rick and Some Hot Chic, 2002 AQHA bay mare, by Master Remedy and out of Colonels Hot Chic by Just Plain Colonel, herd work training.

The cutting pen is set up the same, i.e., using a herd of cattle against the wall in the center of the pen with a herd holder on either side of the herd and two turn-back horses and riders out front.

The reined cow horse herd work is performed in line with a specific discipline style. Horses under the age of 6 either in the snaffle bit or bosal are worked two handed in the herd work or cutting competition. Horses that are 6 years of age are worked in the two-rein or double bridle. Horses over the age of 6 are worked in the bridle or one handed. These showing techniques are the normal when herd work is offered in addition to the rein and fence work in a reined cow horse competition class.

On the other hand, cutting is strictly a one-handed proposition with the rider allowing the horse to work the cow unassisted and without rein direction and working parallel to the cow being worked or cut. In this event, the rider maintains balance with the aid of the saddle horn with the free hand while the rein hand is descended on the horse's neck or resting on the saddle, with the horse working on a free rein.

Notwithstanding, I start both horses on cattle exactly the same. I bring my colts and fillies into the training barn in January of their 2-year-old year no matter what month they were born in. All of my training starts in the round pen. I like a round pen of approximately 100 feet in width as a minimum.

In the round pen, the young horse is broke to the saddle and riding. The horse stays in the round pen until the horse can perform spins, walk, jog, canter in both directions, stops and backs up easily and collected, performs rollbacks on the fence and can move its front end and shoulders left and right with ease.

One of the paramount training techniques that the round pen is indispensable for is teaching the horse to roll back over its hocks and change directions at the trainer's discretion. The most important component of this training technique begins with having the young horse stop and turn into the wall of the round pen to change directions without a rider which allows the youngster to learn to stop, take a step back, roll over its hocks into the round pen wall, and move its shoulders out of the way which is essential to working and cutting a cow.

Once the youngster is proficient in performing this exercise, the same exercise is duplicated while under saddle with a rider. When performing this training exercise, never allow the horse to learn to turn away from the wall to change directions. This promotes a barrel racing turn that is "taboo" and instills a bad habit in the horse.

When I can ride the horse in all of the above training phases and the horse is supple in the face, then I move out to the main arena to continue training until I have sufficient control over the horse to duplicate the same training exercises outlined in the round pen with ease.

Starting Your Horse On A Flag:

The next phase of training involves utilization of the electric cow or Pro Cutter. In my opinion, this is one of the most valuable training tools a cow horse can be subjected to in preparing for either the cutting or reined cow horse pen. The advantages of this training tool is that the trainer can duplicate instances where the young horse is having problems which the trainer may or may not be able to duplicate while working a cow in the pen. The Pro Cutter allows the problem to be duplicated until the action can be corrected.

My technique for working a cow horse on a cow is to have the horse step into the cow at a 45-degree angle to stop the cow. When the cow changes direction, I step my horse back and allow him or her to roll over its hocks to remain heads up with the cow. Over time I've found the 45-degree training technique works best for me.

I'm not an advocate of training a horse to perform 180-degree turns to stay heads up with the cow after the stop and turn. In my opinion, from experience, this training technique can cause a myriad of problems, some of which are expensive hock injections and "run offs" when the horse over rotates, loses sight of the cow and panics, knowing a sharp reprimand is sure to follow.

To start my horse on the flag, I move the flag to the center of the arena and position my horse in front of the flag, a considerable distance away, and allow the young horse to simply watch the flag move back and forth the length of the flag line. This training technique allows the young horse to become accustomed to the movement of the flag as well as the sound of the motor of the Pro Cutter.

Chelsi Guillory and Some Hot Chic faced up with the flag, engaged and in focus.

With each training session, I move the young horse closer to the flag with each distance being predicated on the reaction of the horse to the movement and sound of the flag produced by the Pro Cutter. If during this training exercise, the young horse loses his or her attention or focus on the flag, I will stop the flag and step the horse toward the flag until he or she becomes refocused and then I'll reposition the horse.

Once the horse is refocused, I will continue with the training exercise. The important point to remember is to observe your horse and refocus each time it's necessary until the horse remains in focus with the electric flag moving back and forth the full length of the training line. Another main important point to remember is not to bring the training session to a length of time where the horse becomes bored. I usually spend 10 or 15 minutes on this exercise each day I ride the horse.

The final main point to remember is to return the electric flag to the center of the Pro Cutter line length before stopping the exercise, always back your horse away and turn the horse to the right before leaving the flag area.

Blondys Dual Oak and Rick at the end of the run and in the process of backing up, rolling over her hocks and changing direction.

When the young horse accepts the movement of the flag and the sound of the electric motor without spooking away from the flag, I start the exercise by facing the horse with the center of the flag and stepping the horse to the flag until the horse and I are about 10 feet away.

I then start moving the flag from left to right in small increments until I see the ears of the horse pitch forward, which tells me the horse is fully engaged in the exercise.

Then I'll increase the distance until the flag is moving back and forth in a distance of approximately 10 to 15 feet in either direction. Maintaining focus for the horse is paramount and is accomplished by setting the training exercise up the same during each training session.

Chelsi and Some Hot Chic shown changing directions, being parallel with the flag and in focus.

When the flag is centered in the middle of the length of the Pro Cutter training line, step the horse to the flag, back up and repeat until the horse's ears pitch forward, which is a sign the horse is focused.

At this point, move the flag in either direction and coax the horse to move with the flag on as much of a parallel line as possible at a distance of six to ten feet away. When the flag stops, bring the horse to a stop. I start backing the horse up and after he takes one or two steps, I bring the flag toward the horse.

When the flag reaches the center of the horse, I move the horse's frontend in the direction of the flag and allow the horse to remain parallel and heads up with the flag without employing too much training. Remember the purpose at this point is allowing the horse to gain confidence and learn to move with the flag on its own and without too much coaxing from the rider.

Remember, the inside hand or hand closest to the flag is your direction hand and is used to keep the horse's head and eye in contact with the flag while the outside hand or off hand is used to control the speed of the horse, stop the horse and initiate the backup and roll over the hocks to change directions.

Once the horse can work the flag with ease and perform all of the required training, i.e., moving freely with the flag on his or her own as well as remaining in focus while stopping, starting and turning with the flag, the horse is ready to begin work with cattle.

Starting Your Horse on Cattle:

At this point, I like to bring my young horses to the training pen and just let them stand and watch everything that's going on. Remember, your dealing with a young horse and everything is new to them; therefore, everything, including the training activity of horses working, the sights and sounds of the cows and the entire episode, involves allowing the young horse to accustom his or herself to this activity prior to working cattle.

The next step in starting the young horse on cattle is actually working the horse in the cow pen without actually working a cow until the horse becomes accustomed to working around cattle. One of the techniques I use is to put a group of cattle in the arena with the horse and just walking, jogging, and cantering the horse around the pen with the horse being able to visually observe and become accustomed to the cattle.

Dennis on Dual N For Me, a 2-year-old stallion sired by Dualin Oak, working a single cow on the wall of the cutting pen during a one-on-one training exercise

Normally during this exercise the cattle will spread out all over the arena allowing the young horse to come in contact with them further allowing the young horse to become accustomed to the new working environment while being in contact with cattle.

When the young horse is relaxed in the cutting pen with the cattle, the next step is to actually work the horse on a cow. At this point, I bring one cow in the arena with the horse to familiarize the horse actually working a cow.

When the young horse can handle the cow on a one-on-

one exercise while moving freely and on its own, as well as tracking, stopping, starting and turning on a cow, it's time to accustom the horse to the herd of cattle. I begin this exercise by placing the cattle in the center of the arena and bunched up.

The next step is actually pushing a cow out of the herd and allowing the horse to move freely on the cow on its own.

Dual N For Me and Dennis cutting a cow out of the herd.

Next I walk the horse around the cattle in either direction until the horse is settled and then I gradually maneuver the horse through the herd until I can walk the horse through the entire herd without incident. If the horse balks, I stop the horse back him or her out of the herd and start the entire exercise over until the horse walks freely through the herd without intimidation.

Once the horse can cut a cow out of the herd with ease, the next step is cutting a cow out of the herd and initiating refining the training of the cow horse in the cutting pen.

At this point, the cow horse can be further refined with training for either the cutting pen or reined cow horse arena. With multiple-event horses, I have a rule in training and exhibition practices. My reined cow horses are shown in cutting and reining first and reined cow horse last. The set-up and training techniques are entirely different.

One of the most important aspects of this training exercise is to remember to go with the horse when it's reacting and freely moving on a cow without too much control until the horse gains sufficient confidence to continue advanced training in either reined cow horse or cutting competition. Confidence is the key to success. Allowing the horse to gain confidence on his or her own with a minimal amount of handling will produce a horse that actually loves its work and playing with a cow is a treat.

Dualin Dude, a 3-year-old gelding sired by Dualin Oak, and Dennis during cutting training.

In the end, the horse should have sufficient confidence and training to handle working cattle in the

102

training discipline he or she is trained in.

The most important aspect I can impart to the reader is that once I have the horse working cattle where I want him or her, I perform more training on the electric flag or Pro Cutter than I actually do working cattle. This keeps my horses sharp and fresh in either discipline and working cattle periodically is a treat for the horse and breaks up the boredom of other repetitive training exercises.

CHAPTER 10

ADVANCED TRAINING
THE ART OF REINED COW HORSE FENCE WORK

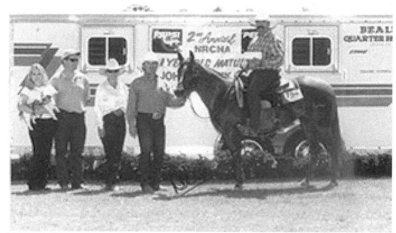

NRCHA Champions and money earners Rick Dennis and Dual Train (NRCHA Snaffle Bit Futurity finals and NRCHA Superior mare sired by Dual Peppy out of Nics Train by Reminic) in the winner's circle at a California NRCHA Cow Horse show.

As a professional reined cow horse trainer, my job is to train the horse and rider in one of the most, if not the most, exciting aspect of the reined cow horse discipline – the cow event. During a student cow horse training class, he or she is taught to perform this event in a disciplined, smooth and controlled manner while exercising caution and safety at all times.

The duality of this event is that on one hand it can be the most exciting if properly executed, but on the other hand it can also be the most dangerous if not properly executed.

The main objective is for the horse and rider to maintain control of the cow and not vice versa. When the cow is in control of the event the experience can quickly become out of control and often times develops into either a poor scoring run or in the worst-case scenario – a high-speed train wreck.

The latter usually happens when the horse and rider are always playing catch up or when they are way behind the cow and out of position.

To avoid both of these scenarios the rider must learn the art and principles of the cow event, develop the discipline to steer his or her horse safely during this maneuver as well as learning how to read a cow to anticipate its movements – with all of this being executed under show conditions in a limited time frame and eventually at a high rate of speed.

I learned the art of reined cow horse on the West Coast at a legendary reined cow horse training facility while exhibiting with the National Reined Cow Horse Association (NRCHA) and absorbing the teachings and showmanship of the great and legendary reined cow horse trainers I became associated with.

From each, I learned a different style and approach to this excellent and exciting sport but from all I learned the "Art of Winning" in each one's unique way in the reined cow horse show pen with the NRCHA.

I still teach these exact training-and-showing methods I learned on the West Coast to my students and instill the same equestrian training techniques and philosophies in my reined cow horses at my training facility – the Wind River Ranch, which was created and developed to carry on and preserve the old style or vaquero training methods.

As I've stated in previous chapters, a cow horse is a cow horse whether a cutter or a reined cow horse. The difference between the two is the manner in which each one is trained, set up and developed in the cutting pen for a specific showing discipline: reined cow horse or cutting. However, each are started on cattle exactly the same.

One of the advantages the cutting participant has over

the reined cow horse participant can be identified in this manner: the cutting participant observes his or her cattle prior to selection and participation while the cow horse participant only sees his or her single cow when it enters the arena after being released through the entry gate.

The cow event is the final event in a National Reined Cow Horse show and is comprised of three (3) components: boxing, fence work and circling. In my opinion, the multiple-event performer or reined cow horse is without equal in the cow horse line, possessing extreme cow sense and trainability while demonstrating the epitome of equine grace, elegance and athleticism.

Rick Dennis and the gelding Dualin Dude, a reining, cutting and cow horse champion and money earner, sired by Dualin Oak out of Stella Peaches, illustrating cow domination in the cutting pen.
Photo by owner Deborah Dutsch Wickham.

BOXING is the first component of the cow event and demonstrates the ability of the horse and rider to control a cow at the end of the arena in a disciplined, smooth and controlled manner without allowing the cow to escape the boxing area. In a very limited time frame, it's important for the rider to evaluate the cow, decide to work it, or call for a new cow and use this time to help his or her horse get completely hooked up and develop a working rhythm.

The first principle I teach my students is to position the horse in an offset position as the cow enters the arena, either right or left, of the cow entry gate instead of meeting the cow head on or being positioned in the front or center of the entry gate.

The purpose of this positioning is three fold: 1) the horse and rider are not directly in front of the cow upon entry which allows an aggressive cow to immediately challenge the horse and roll off the horse's shoulders thus escaping the boxing area, 2) this positioning will allow the rider to observe the cow upon entry and evaluate its temperament and workability factors before actual work begins and 3) the horse and rider can intercept or head the cow at an angle which generally forces the cow against the rail of the boxing area, thus providing the horse and rider with a decisive strategic working advantage by providing a larger target for the cow to maneuver around to escape.

Usually, the speed of the cow can be determined in the boxing area by experimenting with the distance between the horse and rider and the cow once the cow is headed and turned on the wall of the arena. A rule of thumb to remember with some cows is, "the farther away you are the slower they go" but on the other hand, "the closer you are the faster they go." I teach my students to begin evaluating speed control and workability as soon as the cow is headed and positioned on the arena wall.

If the cow is wild or aggressive, I teach my students to simply face the cow and back up until the cow settles down and then resume the boxing when the rider is a safe distance from the cow. Generally, a few steps back is all that's necessary. A telltale sign of a wild cow includes a fast darting motion upon entering the arena with its tail held straight up in the air.

During each passing turn of the cow on the arena wall, I teach my students to close the distance between the horse

107

and rider and the cow, while judging the reaction, speed and temperament of the cow, until an optimal distance is reached where the horse and rider can block the cow on the wall, if possible, and let the horse cut the cow on the wall heads up.

This training procedure is duplicated in the training pen during cutting training and accomplishes three goals: 1) it teaches total domination of the cow by the horse, 2) increases the aggressiveness of the horse working the cow or brightens them up and 3) it allows the horse to develop confidence on its own and teaches a cow horse to anticipate or read a cow's every movement.

However, the main objective of this exercise is to develop and instill an instant sense of respect for the horse and rider by the cow. This should also allow the horse and rider to hopefully maintain control of the cow during the fencing event or bringing the cow down the rail for turns in each direction, as well as the eventual circling of the cow to conclude the cow event.

Over time, I've found the best training exercise to use to develop a student in an exact boxing technique and rhythm is to teach the mechanics of boxing on the Pro Cutter or mechanical cow in advance of working an actual cow in the arena. Each aspect of the correct boxing techniques can be readily executed by the horse and rider on this training device, which in turn will keep the horse in tune and provide valuable working knowledge and confidence for the rider.

During this training exercise, the student will learn how to apply leg pressure to the horse to move the horse in or away from the cow (side pass), which will duplicate the procedure used later on during the fence work event. This training exercise on the Pro Cutter also teaches the student the exact techniques and positioning necessary for a successful stopping and turning of a cow on the rail in each direction when markers are placed in specific locations adjacent to the flag.

FENCE WORK involves the actual release of the cow from the boxing area by the horse and rider and driving the cow down the wall in a disciplined, smooth and controlled manner to negotiate the required turns on the rail.

The setup for this maneuver is accomplished during the boxing portion of the event. I instruct my students to depart the boxing area from the opposite end of the arena, with the head of the horse on the hip of the cow and as close as possible to the cow when he or she decides to depart the boxing area and bring the cow down the rail. The ideal scenario is for the cow to reach the opposite end of the arena, make the turn onto the rail and continue traveling straight down the rail with the horse and rider maintaining control of the cow at all times.

The student is taught to adjust his or her speed with the cow as it travels down the rail in order to maintain a head-to-hip position. In advance of executing this maneuver, I train my cow horses in two vital concepts: 1) to respect and listen to the feel of my bridle hand cues and 2) to learn that

Rick shown riding Dual N For Me performing cow horse training while displaying the perfect head-to-hip alignment used to teach a cow horse to bring a cow down the fence in a reined cow horse class.

I can take the cow horse off the cow anytime I want to. These training concepts are vital to the safety of the horse and rider.

To accomplish both of these goals, I track a single cow in the cutting pen while applying the head-to-hip training technique. If during the tracking, the horse begins lugging on the bridle and trying to take the bridle reins away from me or becomes to aggressive with the cow, I apply bridle rein pressure in a gradual phase until I can bring the cow horse to a stop, back it up and resume the tracking exercise.

However, I never jerk a horse in the ground, which causes other training issues. If the cow horse reaches a point where I want to change the position of the horse in relation to the cow and he or she won't listen to my cues, I stop the horse, spin it away from the cow, immediately put it back on the cow and resume my tracking training once the correction is made.

Another training aid I teach my students is to negotiate the step at the end of the arena, which involves the horse and rider negotiating an imaginary diagonal line across the end of the arena as a short cut to maintain an exact head-to-hip relationship with the cow while leaving the boxing area and traveling down the rail. The rule of thumb is to never travel behind the cow in the end turn or the horse and rider will be playing catch up with the cow, which is not a very good or safe position to be in. Another rule to remember when negotiating this short cut is not to be too far ahead or heads up with the cow or it normally will stop and return to the boxing area.

The head-to-hip scenario is the ideal working position for the horse and rider to maintain control of the cow in a disciplined, smooth and controlled manner while traveling down the rail to negotiate the first high-speed turn, as the horse is accelerated a little past the cow and the cow honors the horse for the stop. As I learned from my West Coast teachings, while traveling down the rail, if you can't reach off the back of the horse and touch the cow you're too far away.

Further, this head-to-hip positioning also negates the horse and rider from having to play catch up and blast past the cow in an attempt to turn it on the rail. This usually results in a miss and a spin around by the horse that provides an ideal position for the cow to strike the horse and rider in a head-on collision. Or in a worst-case scenario, the cow comes off the rail prematurely and cuts in front of and crashes into the horse and rider thus causing a high-speed train wreck by knocking one or both shoulders out from underneath the horse.

A rule of thumb to remember with the head-to-hip positioning is maintaining control of your horse and not allowing the horse to bite the cow while traveling down the rail. I learned this rule by being disqualified during a cow horse show in Arab, Alabama, when my horse Dual Train while traveling down the rail reached out, grabbed the cow by the ear and jerked it to the ground. Lesson learned: No roughing the cow. Next I teach my students to remain cognizant of their surroundings in the arena and remain focused on turning the cow before the end marker to avoid penalties.

A very important factor I teach my students is if for some reason he or she is not comfortable with how a particular cow is working, he or she should exercise extreme caution and safety in this position and scrap the run all together. Sometimes discretion is the better part of valor. In some cases a particular cow can be very dangerous to work and quite simply can't be worked by a horse and rider.

Turning the cow on the rail is not a difficult task if the cow is set up properly and it is a very beautiful display of horsemanship, resulting in long, flowing slides and rooster-tail plumes of arena dirt spewing into the air as the cow horse sits down during the stop, maintains control and turns the cow on the rail.

The mechanics for this maneuver is instilled in the cow horse in the training pen and begins with working the Pro Cutter or mechanical cow. After presenting the cow horse to the flag heads up and allowing the horse to cut the flag from side to side, I maneuver the horse in a parallel position along side the Pro Cutter in a two-handed snaffle bit teaching the horse to look at and track the flag at all times.

I use my outside hand to control the speed, stops and rollbacks of the horse, while my inside hand or the hand closest to the flag, is used as my direction hand. When I'm ready to stop, I ease back on the outside hand to bring the cow horse to a stop as the flag stops, while maintaining enough pressure with the inside hand for the horse's head to maintain eye contact with the flag during the stop. When the flag stops, the horse stops.

Without hesitation, I send the flag in the opposite direction and simultaneously begin the backup using the outside hand and bridle rein to help negotiate the rollback, while applying my inside leg to the inside hip of the cow to push it to the outside and out of the way in order to negotiate a smooth rollback and direction change on the flag.

Once the rollback is completed, I swap hand positioning and the maneuver is completed in the opposite direction with my horse maintaining perfect positioning. This training is performed at the No. 25 position of my speed control or in a very slow manner and repeated until the horse knows to back up and turn in the proper manner.

Once the horse is accomplished with this maneuver, I move to the rail of the arena without the flag and duplicate it at a walk, jog and lope. I repeat this until the horse knows when pressure is applied with the outside hand and his or her head is turned into the rail simultaneously during the stop, a rollback is about to be completed. After awhile it becomes automatic for the horse to perform this maneuver and he will be the same when turning the cow on the rail.

During this exercise, the rule of thumb to remember is a cow horse has to be on the correct lead while traveling down the fence with a cow in order to negotiate a straight and smooth controlled stop, as well as after coming out of the rollback and traveling in the opposite direction. If traveling to the right and rolling to the left, the horse has to be on the left lead coming out of the rollback. If traveling to the left and rolling to the right, the horse has to be on the right lead coming out of the rollback.

Rick and Dual Train performing their first turn on the rail. Note: The cow horse is stopping straight, the cow is on the wall and the cow horse is on the correct lead for the stop with the outside leg extended.
Photo by Dana Photography

This becomes more paramount when stopping a cow on the rail. If a horse is on the correct lead, the horse generally uses the outside leg as a break, which allows the horse to

113

stop straight alongside the cow and not kick the hip out and around to the outside which places the horse and rider in a very bad position.

If the horse is on the incorrect lead prior to the stop, the horse usually kicks its hip out and around which produces an undesirable barrel-turn stop and allows the cow to escape either back down the rail ahead of the horse and rider, thus placing the horse and rider in a catch-up position. Or the cow shoots out the back of the cow horse which requires the horse and rider to perform a loop around to place the cow back on the rail for the next stop and turn.

Rick and Dual Train executing their second turn on the rail. Note: How the cow attempted to jump over the horse and rider and Dual Train bent around the cow to completely block it – but the cow is still on the rail
Photo by Dana Photography

The ideal and most desirable concept is to use the head-to-hip relationship to control the speed of the cow down the rail, set the cow up for the stop and turn by accelerating just a little ahead of the cow.

After the stop and turn, this ideal positioning allows the horse and rider to remain in an ideal working position to bring the cow back down the rail for the next set of stops and turns. Generally, when a horse arrives even with or a little ahead of the cow, the animal will stop and try to escape by backing out behind the horse and traveling in the opposite direction.

One of the main components I teach my students to use is the head-to-hip relationship to form a funnel, with my outside leg being used as a break while moving the horse closer to the cow while accelerating to the head. This squeezes the cow on the rail and forces the stop in a disciplined, smooth and controlled manner. This is the safest way to stop a cow traveling at a high rate of speed and should be used instead of running down the arena and cutting in front of the cow for the stop.

Rick and Dual Train demonstrating the proper cow circling technique.
Photo by Dana Photography

After the stop, the cow has been removed from the rail toward the center of the arena. The horse and rider have taken the short route to head and turn the cow with horse

115

and rider in perfect position to drive up and around the cow to execute the next circling phase of the event.

I teach my students to perform three turns on the rail if at all possible: one on each end and one in the middle of the arena to bring the cow off the wall to begin circling the cow once in each direction.

CIRCLING is the last maneuver in the cow event and requires the cow being removed from the wall and circling it one time in each direction. This action is preferably negotiated as close to the middle of the arena as possible.

During my third stop, I use my outside leg to maneuver the horse in between the arena wall and the cow thus forcing the cow to leave this area, which usually sends it out toward the center of the arena. Once the cow leaves the area, I teach my students to take the short route to head the cow to begin the circling process. In simplicity, if the cow is traveling to the left, intercept and head the cow on the left. If the cow is traveling to the right, intercept and head the cow on the right.

If the opposite is performed, the horse and rider are taking the long route to circle the cow. This can rapidly deplete the horse's remaining energy level, which is necessary for class completion, and in some cases the horse and rider could fail to negotiate two successful circles of the cow.

Each of my cow horse students are taught when circling a cow to remain as close to the cow as possible but once again, the circling distance is strictly predicated on the temperament and work ability of the cow and this distance can only be judged and attained by the rider during execution of the maneuver.

A rule of thumb to remember is: when the cow is headed and turned by the horse and rider, to begin the circling of the cow, he or she must continue to use the outside leg to drive the horse up and around the cow. If

116

during this process the horse and rider fail to achieve this goal, the cow is again placed in the driver's seat with the horse and rider playing catch up. Sometimes this is a very precarious place to be in.

One of the best lessons I learned in this great sport is that a cow can outmaneuver a horse and to be successful in the sport of cow horse, the rider must master the use of angles in the show pen to achieve success safely.

CHAPTER 11

ADVANCED TRAINING
TRANSITIONING FROM THE SNAFFLE
BIT TO THE BOSAL

Dual Train, the NRCHA Bosal/Hackamore finalist

A bosal is a type of noseband used on the classic hackamore of the vaquero tradition. It is usually made of braided rawhide and is fitted to the horse in a manner that allows it to rest quietly until the rider uses the reins to give a signal. It acts upon the horse's nose and jaw. Over the horse's nose the bosal has a thick, stiff wrapper, called a "nose button." Beneath the horse's chin, the ends of the bosal are joined at a heavy heel knot. The bosal is carried on the animal's head by a headstall, sometimes called a "bosal hanger."

The rein system of the hackamore is called the mecate. The mecate is a long rope, traditionally of horsehair, approximately 20–25 feet long, tied to the bosal in a specialized manner that adjusts the fit of the bosal around the muzzle of the horse and creates both a looped rein and a long free end that can be used for a number of purposes. When a rider is mounted, the free end is usually tied to the saddle horn to keep it out of the way and is not used to tie the horse to a solid object, but rather is used as a lead rope and a form of Longe line when needed.

Photo Courtesy of Steve Guitron, Custom Rawhide Vista, California

The bosal is ridden with two hands, and uses direct

119

pressure, rather than leverage. It is particularly useful for encouraging flexion and softness in the young horse, though it has a design weakness in that it is less useful than a snaffle bit for encouraging lateral flexion.

There are two different applications use for the bosal: The classic Vaquero and modern practitioners of the "California" cowboy tradition started a young horse in a bosal hackamore. Over time they moved to even-thinner and lighter bosals (bosalito), then added a spade bit and eventually transitioning to a spade alone, ridden with romal style reins, often retaining a light "bosalito" without a mecate. This process took many years and required an expert trainer.

The "Texas" tradition cowboy, and most modern trainers, will often start a young Western riding horse in a bosal, but then move to a snaffle bit and then to a simple curb bit. They may never introduce the spade at all. Other trainers start a horse with a snaffle bit, then once lateral flexion is achieved, they move to a bosal to encourage flexion and then transition to a curb. However, this sequence is frowned upon by those who use classic Vaquero techniques.

I learned to train the reined cow horse using the snaffle bit first, the Bosal second, the two-rein or double bridle third and the bridle last. This training style was required to compete in the Cow Horse competition with the National Reined Cow Horse Association (NRCHA).

There's nothing wrong with any of the previous training techniques or examples that use the bosal or hackamore to start a young horse. However, my personal preference is to start with the snaffle bit and split reins because I get more lateral flexion than I do with the bosal.

Over time, its been my experience certain training techniques have been developed by trainers, in certain geographical locations to meet the demands of the discipline the trainer shows in and trains for.

The main objective to breaking, starting and training a young horse is to do it right in the first place.

Bosal Transition:
Step 1:
By now, your horse should be a completely trained snaffle bit horse, performing in the performance arena and approaching 5 years of age. When I'm ready to transition a horse to the bosal, I go "back to the basics" and introduce the 4-year-old to the training apparatus in the horse's stall. I saddle the youngster, place the colt in the stall with the no-pull halter attached and hook the horse to the tether ring attached to the wall.

As with the introduction of any new training device, I allow the horse to inspect, smell and feel the bosal prior to placing it on the horse. After a few minutes of familiarity time, I bridle the horse with the bosal, just like putting on any other head stall I'm going to use that day. The tip to remember is to place the reins over the horse's head first to allow for a smooth attachment of the bosal over the horse's nose and attach the hanger behind the ears of the horse.

At this point I loop the trailer around the saddle horn a couple of times to move the trailer out of the way. If for any reason the colt resists or becomes alarmed by the bosal, take it off and repeat the steps until the colt settles down and willingly accepts the new training apparatus.

As with all new training concepts, never leave the horse unattended in a stall, or tied up anywhere for that matter, without a watchful eye on the horse during training. If these horses aren't watched, this can be a recipe for disaster!

Once the colt has accepted the bosal, I let the horse stand in the stall in my presence for a few minutes so he can become accustomed to the new training apparatus. Then I remove the headgear and repeat the process until I'm sure the horse has accepted the smell and feel of the

121

new training device.

Step 2:

What I was taught, and what works best for me to initiate the Bosal transition, is to warm the horse up and complete an entire training regimen in the snaffle bit first. When the training is over, I bring the horse to the round pen, remove the headstall with the snaffle bit and replace it with the bosal headstall. I climb in the saddle and begin to walk the colt around the round pen allowing the horse to travel where it wants to without correction. I never use the bosal on a fresh horse!!

When I'm ready to begin accustoming the colt to the bosal, I begin the training exercise in the same fashion as I would if I were riding the colt with a halter and a set of reins attached. I pull and guide the horse's direction with leg and hand cues. If I want the horse to move to the left, I apply left leg pressure and wide left hand and rein cues. If I want the horse to stop and backup, I open my legs and after the stop, I apply gentle backwards rein pressure that will apply direct pressure to the nose and lower jaw of the colt. If you apply the wrong amount of direct pressure, you will no doubt initiate a sore spot on the horse's nose and jaw.

Step 3:

Remember, in order to fully train the colt in the bosal, the rider must start at the beginning, just as if you were training the horse in the snaffle bit. Begin with a walk, jog and lope in the round pen while teaching the colt to make the proper rate transitions during each exercise.

Another important point to remember is even though the colt is fully trained in the snaffle bit, the bosal imparts a different feel to the horse and he has to adjust to what your asking him to do.

Step 4:

Once you can successfully flex and bend the colt, move the colt's front end and hips, negotiate the walk, jog and lope in the round pen, you can move on to the backup, roll backs, proper head collection, spins each direction and counter canter each direction. You can now move out of the round pen and perform the same exercises in the open arena. Save the flying lead changes, the in-line lead changes and high-speed run downs and stops for last or when you have full control of the colt while performing the previous maneuvers.

The main point to remember is while performing high-speed run downs and the colt starts to pick up speed without you asking for the speed transition, stop, backup and begin the maneuver again and repeat until the colt waits for the speed increase by a request from the rider.

Step 5:

The last phase of training involves preparatory training exercises in advance of working cattle. The best training tool to use for this application is the electric cow or flag.

To properly execute this maneuver, turn to the Chapter 9 "Starting Young Horses on Cattle From a Multi-Event Trainer's Viewpoint" and repeat the identical training methods used in the snaffle bit in the bosal/hackamore.

Step 6:

When your colt is successfully working the electric flag, it's time to move to the cattle arena to begin working cattle. The easiest way to start working cattle is to begin with one cow in the round pen and graduate to a herd of cattle only after you and your colt are proficient with working the single cow with the bosal.

Save the two-handed cutting for last and this will provide you with ample time to acquire your balance with the colt wearing the bosal.

123

Rick's student Joliet Gasquet enjoying "Lil Red" as a finished bosal horse.

The bosal is my favorite training device. Over time I've learned to appreciate the simplicity of the design while learning to respect its effectiveness as a training tool. Essentially, when you first employ the use of the bosal, you'll find out exactly how well your training has been with your colt in the snaffle bit but you'll also be rewarded at the end with a horse that is lighter, more responsive and very supple.

Another reward of the bosal is for the horse, plus the horse's mouth, that has been in training and carrying the snaffle bit on a weekly training basis. In my off times, or when I'm not training and riding my own horses, the bosal is the only headgear that I use.

CHAPTER 12

ADVANCED TRAINING
TRANSITIONING FROM THE TWO-REIN
AND INTO THE BRIDLE.

The two-rein consisting of a bosalito, spade bit, and romal rein.

To transition a horse trained in the bosal to the two-rein, I install the bosalito instead of the bosal prior to executing a training exercise. Even though the bosalito is smaller in diameter, the horse generally accepts it and responds in the same manner as when using the larger diameter bosal.

Step 1:
Once the colt is accustomed to being worked in the bosalito, I add the headstall with the spade bit attached over the bosalito and attach the romal reins to the spade bit head stall, with the reins ending up on the back of the horse's neck. At first your going to think, "What in the world do I

do now and which one do I grab first?"

Katie Wickham and Canadian Blended, Louisiana State Youth Reining Champions, shown as a finished bridle horse with romal reins and a cow horse bit, in perfect form.

The easiest trick to understanding the two-rein concept is to place the romal reins over the saddle horn at the end of the "V" and bring the bosalito reins up through the romal reins and drape them on top of the romal reins.

When you're ready to get in the saddle, grab the bosalito reins in one hand to control the horse while mounting up in the saddle. Once in the saddle, place the bosalito reins in the off hand, grab the romal reins in the other hand and make a fist with the romal reins resting comfortably in the hand with the knuckles facing forward with the thumb resting on top of the knuckle of the first finger.

Next make a loop in the bosalito, slightly open the first finger and place the bosalito loop over the two fingers next to the first finger and close your fist. Apply enough pressure to prevent the bosalito reins from sliding. To adjust the romal reins, pick them up and bring them back toward your chest until your wrist touches your chest. Adjust the romal reins either in or out during traveling to acquire the proper rein extension. Next tighten the bosalito reins so that the bosalito engages the horse's nose first, ahead of bit contact with the spade bit.

To effectively transition the horse, only use the spade bit in case of an emergency. The main focus of the two-rein concept is to allow the horse to become accustomed to the feeling of the romal reins and the spade bit while riding or working. I usually spend a couple of days just pleasure walking the colt in the two-rein prior to actually working the horse in a training environment.

The purpose of this break-in period is to allow the horse to adjust to the feel of the bit in his mouth and become accustomed to the pressure points the bit will engage during training in the bridle. Remember, you will have a horse that is nose sensitive but mouth fresh.

Step 2:

Once the horse is secure and comfortable in the two-rein combination, I start riding him around the arena using a combination of leg and hand cues to control the direction. This teaches the horse to respond to the outside rein pressure. If the horse doesn't respond to the outside rein pressure, take the bosalito with the off hand and direct the horse in the direction you're attempting to travel in. I prefer to use a combination of direction changes in circles rather than attempting other types of direction changes.

I also make sure my rein hand is assisting my leg cue by moving my bridle hand slightly across the horse's neck to the outside of my circle, which tips the horse's nose to the inside. When you're circling in the opposite direction, move the rein hand, romal rein, and bosalito rein across the horse's neck to aid in tipping the horse's nose to the inside of the traveling direction. With enough practice, the horse will become accustomed to this training stimulus and respond accordingly.

Just as the hackamore is the second step in teaching a horse to respond to outside rein pressure, the two-rein is the first step in making a finished bridle horse by adding an additional condition response stimuli. The two-rein concept is a traditional training tool and indispensable in the bridle horse-training book. Once the horse is proficient at responding to outside rein pressure in all directions, it's time to add more to the program.

Before adding more to your training regimen I like to conduct the following training exercise:

"When I lay the reins gently across the neck of a standing horse, his nose should tip to the outside of the rein pressure without moving his body - only his head and neck. If for some reason the horse doesn't readily respond to this training stimulus, I reach over and take the bosalito rein and add a small amount of additional pressure until the horse responds. This is one training concept you should repeat over and over again to accustom the horse to responding to the pressure of the inside rein, which not only aids in direction but increases flexion in the horse.

"The horse must respond to the training stimuli in the same manner as it did in the snaffle bit and the bosal before transitioning to the straight-up bridle and spade bit, as well as executing every required maneuver in the rein work, herd work and fence work. Also, the horse must be bent in the turns the same degrees he was in the two previous training segments in the snaffle bit and the bosal."

Step 3:
When the horse is operating in the two-rein with very little adjustments with the bosalito and is responding to the rider's training hand and leg cues, it's time to start the transition into the bridle. To begin this transition, I readjust my reins to allow small pressure increments with the romal reins and the spade bit while decreasing the pressure with the bosalito until the horse is operating with the romal reins and the spade bit. I train the horse in this manner until I experience very little times when I'm reinforcing a missed training cue with the bosalito.

When I'm ready to ride and train the horse in the straight up bridle, I saddle the horse, leave the bosalito off, put on the headstall with the spade bit and romal reins, go ride and start the training all over again. One important point to remember is that in order for the spade bit to be legal, it must have a bit connector attached to the two shanks at the bottom.

Remember, it takes a lot of time, repetition and patience to train a horse. In the end, you will be rewarded with one of your most valuable treasures - a finished bridle horse.

CHAPTER 13

ADVANCED TRAINING
BACK TO BASICS

One of the most-often-asked questions I receive from readers visiting Rick's Corner at allaboutcutting.com, pertains to the correct manner and steps required, as well as the ones that I use, to return a show horse to competition after a lengthy layoff from the show arena, either due to an injury layup or for any other reason.

When answering this question, I'll use excerpts from my book *"The American Horse Industry – Avoiding the Pitfalls,"* as well as one of my training horses as an example. Some Hot Chic, sired by Master Remedy out of Colonels Hot Chic by Just Plain Colonel, was recently returned to me after an extended four-year layoff. In the former owner's own words, the extended layup is justified in this manner. "Rick, I laid this horse off because I was tired of winning on her!"

To offer some background on Some Hot Chic or Cali, as she is affectionately called by her new owner, she was bred by the Ward Ranch, Inc., Tulare, Calif. She was trained and shown by the Ward Ranch, Inc. as a 3-year-old in the reined cow horse events in the snaffle bit. She was exhibited in the National Reined Cow Horse Association (NRCHA) Snaffle Bit Futurity as well as other NRCHA events afterwards, becoming an NRCHA money earner.

Cali was purchased by the Wind River Ranch as a 5-year-old and trained by me in the Vaquero reined cow horse training disciplines consisting of the bosal, two-rein (double bridle) and bridle.

Upon completion of her training, Cali was sold to her new owner and the pair secured AQHA championships and circuit championships in reining and cow horse. The remarkable aspect of this team's pairing is the owner who, prior to owning this horse, never won a competition title in the show arena during his 20-some-years show career.

Novice reined cow horse exhibitor Chelsi Hankins Guillory, Kentwood, La., purchased Some Hot Chic, nicknamed Cali, in February 2013 and she went into Rick Dennis' Wind River Ranch's "Back To Basics" reconditioning program.

131

While exhibiting from the ranch, the equine team won at will, which undoubtedly accounted for his previous remark and Cali's extended four-year layup.

In February 2013, the mare was sold to her new owner and novice reined-cow-horse exhibitor Chelsi Hankins Guillory, Kentwood, La. After the mare's purchase, she was placed back with the Wind River Ranch training program and required a complete reconditioning program – which meant that the new equine team went "Back To Basics."

The first step that I take in evaluating the physical condition of an equine athlete returning to training after an extended layup, transpires in the round pen. I begin working the horse in the round-pen environment with an initial workout lasting only five minutes or so. All the while, I am evaluating the horse's breathing and stamina condition by using a rotating combination exercise regimen consisting of walk, trot and canter.

I use this exercise regimen on a daily basis and add five-minute increments until the horse can perform all of the combination exercises for a maximum of 15 minutes per session. All the while, the horse should be exhibiting no signs of excess breathing or physical exhaustion. As a precautionary measure, the reader should be aware that I never add more time to a horse's conditioning exercise regimen until the horse can easily perform the allotted time without undue stress or stamina (physiological) limitations.

As one legendary West Coast reined cow horse trainer and NRCHA Hall of Fame inductee once stated, "A horse is an athlete that must be trained physically, spiritually and mentally."

The other aspect of this well-spoken advice is to consider that an equine athlete is no different from any other athlete when subjected to physical training. Specific care must be taken to muscle, ligament, tendon, joint and mental conditioning. Therefore, equine safety equipment is a must, i.e. splint and bell boots. Further, a horse's specific diet is directly related to physical conditioning and should consist of a diet rich in nutrition, including vitamins, nutrients, fat and protein content which are required for rapid muscle, tendon and ligament conditioning.

As an added precaution, I introduce a joint supplement to every horse's diet that is in training to replenish joint fluid depletion during exercise, as well as electrolytes when necessary.

Once the horse is physically fit for a 15-minute sustained work out in the round pen, the horse is saddled and reintroduced to riding under saddle in the main arena. My initial workout regimen consists of a "three-and-two" workout schedule: three days riding and two days off.

After a horse has been in Dennis' retraining regimen, the horse is worked through its entire familiar and former training regimen. Shown is Chelsi riding Cali on a cow

133

The important component to remember in equine conditioning is that the horse is trained and merely requires physical conditioning and a tune-up to achieve showing capability. Therefore, conduct the physical conditioning slow and easy.

Another important component in my retraining regimen is to start the horse off in the snaffle bit and work my way back up to the desired working bit that will be used when someone is showing the horse – thus, returning "Back To Basics" and working the horse through its entire familiar and former training regimen.

One of the basics I've learned is not to induce any training to the horse until it's physically and mentally prepared, or approximately 30 days into the retraining program. This is sufficient time for the horse's tendons, ligaments, joints and muscles to adjust to the reintroduction of training.

Experience has taught me that an equine-athlete reconditioning and retraining program requires a minimum of 90 days to achieve a peak-performance level prior to reentering equine competition in the show arena.

My initial under-saddle retraining exercises take place in a standard 100 X 200 regulation arena and consist of one walk each direction, one extended trot each direction and one canter each direction. These beginning exercises are repeated each day during the specified training time period, or "three-and-two" work-out schedule, and are not increased until the equine athlete can perform these basic exercises in a proficient and non-impaired physical manner.

My goal is to add one addition to each of the above exercises until a maximum of three walk-trot-canter exercises are able to be performed by the horse without physical limitation.

Since my horses are reined cow horses, requiring performance in a multiple-event category, i.e., reining, cutting and cow horse, I alternate training exercises during

134

each training session. The most indispensable training tool that I use during the stock-horse retraining – besides my bits, bosal and bridle – is the electric cow or Pro Cutter. This is a multi-facet tool that I use to retrain my stock horses but at the same time train students in various aspects of cow work, which prepares them for their actual introduction to working a live cow.

The most indispensable tool that Dennis uses to train the stock horse is the Pro Cutter Electric Cow. Chelsi is shown riding Cali on the Pro Cutter flag.

At the end of the retraining session, the stock horse should be sufficiently reconditioned and retrained to enter the competition arena as a fit competitor, which usually results in a more competitive, well-rested athlete after an extended lay up.

The photographs in this article depict Some Hot Chic and Chelsi during their training and showing phase, which resulted in the equine team receiving money earnings, four Championships and one Reserve Championship in their first two shows with the Louisiana Stock Horse Association in reining, cutting and cow horse.

Rick and Dualin Oak shown in the bosal.

CHAPTER 14

ADVANCED TRAINING
THE ART OF WINNING

For the novice equestrian, winning in the show arena can be difficult and complex to understand and achieve but over time the new comer with the right tutorship will soon learn this fine art is acquired by repetition in the show pen from show experience, show seasoning and devoted repetitive practice.

How I've achieved my goals with my stock and students through time is one of the most often asked questions I have received. My answer is simple and mimics my company motto. At the Wind River Ranch "Champions are made the old-fashioned way: by hard work, great stock, honest competition and one at a time!"

One of the basic principles I impart to my new students is an old adage, "Winners never quit and quitters never win!" At some point in all of our lives and careers, we've all heard this old saying and it's just as important in the equestrian show arena.

An important aspect of my indoctrination to new students is simple: "If you can't be devoted to your horse and your equestrian discipline, you've picked the wrong sport!"

Save yourself a lot of money by picking another sport to participate in!

Half-hearted attempts won't make it; only repeated failure will follow. In fact and in reality, properly learning to ride a horse is difficult enough for the novice but learning to ride a horse, as well as learning three equestrian disciplines that are comprised of the reined cow horse industry, i.e., reining, cutting and cow horse, makes it even more problematic

Melissa Wickham of Katelissa Performance Horses, Bush, La., shown with Blondys Dualin Oak (Dualin Oax Stella Peaches x Blondys Dude) Top 5 in Youth Walk Trot on her first time out.

Regardless of the equestrian discipline a student decides on, the most important aspect is being devoted to his or her specific type of discipline, the horse and staying mentally focused. What I impart to my students is to pick a certain number of days and amount of time during the week for practice that works around his or her work, parenting or social structure and sticking to this schedule on a devoted basis.

However, when you arrive at practice, be physically and mentally prepared (focused) to learn your discipline and riding techniques, give 100 percent each time you practice and never give up or quit regardless of how hard the maneuvers become. There's no replacement for practice, whether it's rain or shine – hot or cold.

Another important aspect of my training techniques is to make my students aware that the simple mistakes he or she makes routinely during practice will most likely be unconsciously repeated and executed in the equestrian arena on show day. Therefore, make every attempt to practice 100 percent mistake-free each time a lesson is provided by your trainer.

This mental focusing will eventually evolve into mistake-free lessons and will help the student achieve his or her goal of success in the winner's circle on show day by executing mistake-free maneuvers during the run. There should be an understanding between trainer and student that addresses a student's complete understanding of a maneuver before attempting it. If a student doesn't completely understand the principles of the execution of a maneuver prior to execution, he or she should not attempt it until a thorough understanding exists between trainer and student. There's no excuse for not asking enough questions!

As the old saying goes, "There is never enough practice. Practice makes perfect!"

By practicing mistake-free practice maneuvers, the student will soon learn another one of my important lecture topics: in the show pen don't beat yourself by going off course and executing mistakes in a pattern. Make the competitors in your class beat you fair and square. It's better to be beaten by honest competition than being beaten by yourself.

To the novice, show day and the show arena can be a very intimidating place to be but enough practice to the point a specific maneuver is routine, will certainly diminish the odds of the exhibitor going off course during the class. Preparation is the key!

One of the most difficult lessons for a novice equestrian student to learn is that winning and losing go hand in hand in the show pen. Normally, before a student can win, he or she has to go through a trial-and-error period where mistakes are made, classes are lost and, generally speaking, frustration and embarrassment sets in. What I say to my student at this point is, "I'm very proud of you for your competition in the class. Mistakes were made but we all learn from our mistakes so let's capitalize on this learning curve, practice harder, overcome these glitches in our program and move forward to the road of success.

Danetta Comeaux, Metairie, La., with (left) WR Masters Lady (Master Remedy x Peppys First Lady x Peppy San Badger) and Dual Peps Taffy (Mr Dual Pep x Sugar Babes Taffy x Sugar Vandy) who qualified for the AQHA World Show in Amateur Cow Horse and was State Amateur Reining and Cow Horse Champion

The absolute last thing an equestrian student wants to hear or entertain after a disaster in the show pen, is open chastising by a trainer after the class. After all, competing and having fun on your horse is what it's all about – not listening to your trainer rip you up for making mistakes. There's a time and place for a critique of a student's run but show day and the show arena is most assuredly not it.

More times than not, the student is well aware of his or her mistake and doesn't need to be reminded of it at this time and juncture in his or her show career. My job as a trainer is not to chastise but encourage the student, analyze the run and correct the mistake during practice so the mistake doesn't occur during future show attempts.

I encourage my students to enter open or entry-level shows before engaging in a show for registered horses for a number of reasons: 1) open shows are generally comprised of competitors of all levels and are cheaper to compete in and 2) I use these shows for my students to practice, gain confidence and seasoning in rather than allowing them to enter the registered show right out of the gate which are generally comprised of more experienced and seasoned competitors.

Once the new competitor has reached a level of seasoning and confidence, which is displayed in mistake-free class competition, then - and only then - will I encourage him or her to move up to registered shows. While they are at registered shows, I encourage my students to pay close attention to the more seasoned competitors and analyze their runs to learn from. Most students will gain valuable experience during this observation time.

The student needs to learn that he or she must move up to the next level of competition in order to better his or herself competitively. The student must also learn that better competition makes him or her a better competitor. However, if a student enters this competition level ahead of time, more often than not, the student is discouraged rather than encouraged.

The single most important aspect of winning in the equestrian show arena is being prepared to show. The next important aspects of winning encompass mental focus and practice, practice, practice, practice. Equestrian show arena seasoning brings success, quieted nerves, less stomach butterflies, brain loss and more fun with the horse.

Rick showing Ms Cougarette, a daughter of Master Remedy and full sister to Some Hot Chic, on cattle.

CHAPTER 15

NATIONAL REINED COW HORSE ASSOCIATION MULTIPLE-EVENT CLASSES

In a previous chapter, I touched on what's required of your horse and yourself during participation in a National Reined Cow Horse show. This chapter will further your education in this remarkable equine sport by broadening the terminology and execution requirements for successful participation.

The first event of a three-event cow horse show begins with the Herd Work:

Herd Work is similar to cutting but allowing and requiring different showing techniques, i.e., working with two hands instead of one as well as specific training equipment coinciding with the age of the horse being shown. A herd of cattle usually consists of 30 head positioned at the end of the arena and commonly referred to as a "bunch of cattle."

In the arena with you are four equestrian teams, i.e., horse and rider teams consisting of two teams positioned on each side of the "bunch of cattle" next to the arena wall and commonly referred to as" herd holders." In the front of the cattle are two equestrian teams positioned on either side of the "bunch of cattle" and commonly referred to as "turn backs."

The "herd-holders" job is to keep the cattle bunched up on the arena wall in preparation for working by the contestant. The "turn backs" job is to help the rider by: 1) turning back or controlling the flow of cattle pushed out of the herd, by the exhibitor, toward the "turn backs," enabling the exhibitor to select a cow to work from the separated cattle from the bunched herd, 2) Initiate the flow of remaining cattle back to the bunched herd and 3) keeping the cow in the work zone or free position, i.e., between the bunched herd and the "turn backs' " position, enabling the rider to cut or separate the cow from the herd and demonstrate the athleticism and "cow sense" of the horse by not allowing the cow to return to the herd prematurely.

Rick & Dual Train cutting out of the herd at the NRCHA Derby, Medford, Oregon, two handed in the snaffle bit.

After separation, the "turn backs" maintain control of the cow being worked in the work zone until the rider either decides to quit this cow, the horse and rider loses the cow and it returns to herd prematurely, or until the whistle blows signaling the end of the working time period. Each contestant will have two-and-a-half minutes to work cattle to demonstrate the horse and rider's ability to enter a herd of cattle quietly, separate a cow for working and control each cow selected from returning to the "bunched herd" until the work time expires. Usually, a typical herd work demonstration consists of working two or more cows from the "bunched herd" but is dependant on a particular cow's working ability. However, it's imperative for the equestrian team to make at least one deep cut in the "bunched herd" prior to quitting the Herd Work portion of the three-phase event.

Scoring:
1) During the Herd Work demonstration, the equestrian team is judged on its ability to work the cow, herd entrance and exit, eye appeal, difficulty in working the cow, etc. The judge or judges may add or subtract points from the exhibition, which provides a cumulative total for a final performance score for the event.

In the event of multiple judges, i.e. five judges, the high and the low scores are thrown out and the three remaining scores are averaged for a cumulative working score total.

2) Penalties are assessed to the horse and rider for violations committed during the performance, i.e., prematurely quitting a cow (hot quit), loss of working advantage (miss), lost cow (cow returns to the herd prematurely, horse turns away from the cow, herd entrance and exit), flushing the herd (disturbing the herd while working, rider falling off the horse, etc.)

3) Abuse or lameness receives a no score.

Rein Work is similar to reining, except the rider may exhibit the horse with two hands instead of one, i.e., snaffle bit or bosal. Two-rein classes require one hand on the rein but permit any number of fingers between the reins. Unlike other reining classes, there are no rollback requirements during exhibition. Bridle classes are strictly a one-handed requirement. The equestrian team is judged on their ability to demonstrate the athletic ability of the horse by executing

145

a series of turnarounds (spins) - right and left, lead departures, fast and slow circle transitions, flying lead changes, high speed run downs and stops, back ups as well as eye appeal.

Nic Chex, NRCHA Superior, Rein Work Paso Robles, Calif. Owner is Rick Dennis.

Penalties:
1) Penalties may be assessed for: Going off course (blown pattern), missed lead changes, rider falling off the horse, balking (horse refusing to execute any portion of the maneuver), riders failure to maintain control of the horse, etc.

2) Points may be added or subtracted from the performance by the judges and is dependant upon the accurate execution of the maneuvers.

146

3)   Abuse or lameness receives a no score.

• **Cow Work aka Fence Work:**
The last phase of the multiple-event performance is the
Cow Work aka Fence Work. Chapter 10 describes in detail
the horse-training requirements to perform this event but
also describes in detail how to safely perform this
maneuver while showing. The performance is started upon
entry of a randomly selected cow entering the arena from a
door located in the center of the arena end. Upon entry, the
horse and rider will initiate the maneuver consisting of the
following phases:

• **Phase 1 - Boxing.** The horse and rider must demonstrate
the equestrian team's ability to control the cow in the entry
or boxing area until the rider is ready to bring the cow
down the fence or side wall of the arena to complete the
first turn of the event.

Phase 2 - Fence Turns. After boxing, the equestrian team
must demonstrate its ability to control the cow by moving it
out of the boxing area, travel down the arena wall, stop and
turn the cow before the end marker and bring it back down
the arena wall and complete the second turn.

• **Phase 3 - Circling.** Upon completing the second turn the
equestrian team must demonstrate its ability to remove the
cow from the arena wall, move it to the center of the arena
and circle it once each way, i.e., right and left circles. The
sound of the judge's whistle signifies the end of the
maneuver. The equestrian team may conduct a third turn
before bringing the cow to the middle of the arena to circle
it but care must be exercised or a penalty may be assessed
for exhausting the cow.

Dual Train, NRCHA Superior, and Wendy Ward Lorenco at the NRCHA 1998 Snaffle Bit Futurity in Reno, Nev., circling the cow during the last phase of the "cow or fence work."

1) Each equestrian team performing this maneuver is judged on its ability to control the cow, loss of working advantage, exhausting the cow, not turning cow prior to the designated markers, falling off the horse, etc.

2) It would be advisable for the participant desiring to engage in the performance arena in a reined cow horse competition to obtain a copy of the National Reined Cow Horse Association Rule Book for a complete listing and requirements of each division of showing. This book only delineates the general guidelines to rules and showing but does not contain a complete listing of all of the rules.

3) Abuse and Lameness receives a no score.

CHAPTER 16

KNOW WHEN TO SAY WHEN

If you've reached this chapter of the book, it's my personal opinion that you've reached the most important phase in your education and horse-training success.

"Know When To Say When" is a relative term signifying the most common mistake all horse trainers eventually make, myself included. There is an optimum time to recognize this relative term during training: when you and your horse have performed your jobs in a particular training exercise with expert guidance on your behalf, and an excellent performance on the horses behalf. Instead, you failed to do the next logical and perhaps the most crucial aspect of the training exercise, i.e., "end on a positive note."

Instead of praising your horse and living to fight another day so-to-speak, you ask your horse for one more advancement in another training phase unrelated to the one you and your horse just executed masterly. The next chapter of this training saga produces something you are totally unprepared for and that's a sulking rebellious student - your horse.

Instead of trying to understand the exercise, your horse rebels. A little rebellious nature ends up in a big fight. Tempers flare - yours and the horse. Instead of training to a successful ending, you're concentrating on defusing a brawl in the training arena and trying to quite on a positive note.

Eventually, the above illustration is repeated in every horse trainer's career.

To paraphrase the "Know-When-To-Say-When"

149

concept, visualize the meaning in its entirety or by another interpretation i.e., knowing the exact limitations and capabilities of your horse's athletic ability to perform the maneuver.

The timeframe allotted before your horse reaches its maximum physiological and psychological output exertion level, i.e., quantifying when your horse has reached a training level proficiency enabling it to grasp more than one training exercise at a time.

What I've found that works best for me is to master one training level at a time until I can interface small doses of a myriad of training disciplines into one training session both as a retraining session as well as graduating the horse in mastering specific training maneuvers without mishap. The main point to remember is not to over do it. A horse, like a human, has good days, bad days and its best days. Listen to your horse's attitude on a particular day and adjust your training regimen accordingly.

Best days are when I accomplish a lot with a horse or a student, for that matter. On good days, I concentrate on getting as much accomplished as I can without becoming embroiled in a bad situation with either party. On bad days, I get as much done until my horse or student has reached the "Peter Principle" or when an individual or horse has reached its maximum output level in a given situation without reaching a level of incompetency.

At this point I cut my losses and call it a day. Remember, it's up to the trainer to learn this phenomena both in horses and in individuals in order to enjoy a successful horse training, student training, or professional training career in the equine business. Each trainer's success and failure is dependent on his or her mastery of the "Art of Interpretation" and adjust the training schedule accordingly to promote a successful conclusion. A rule of thumb I live by is; if my horse performs what I'm asking it to do in as little as fifteen minutes I reward the horse by cooling it out and calling it a day thus quitting positively!

Lucy Tetlow and Peppysvegashowgirl, AQHA National Ltd Rider earning a 5th place in Novice Cow Horse, National Stock Horse Association Year End Top 10 and buckle earner in the bridle in Ltd Open Cow Horse, MSRHA/NRHA Reining Champion and money earner. She was also a champion and money earner in reining, cutting, and cow horse at the stock shows. Vegas was trained by Rick as a 2-year old in the snaffle bit and completed her training in the bosal, two-rein and bridle.

CHAPTER 17

REINED COW HORSE - THE VERSATILITY CHAMPION

Chelsi Guillory and Some Hot Chic, barrel Racing champions and money earners.

The most important qualities of the California Stock Horse is its athletic ability, speed, strength, mind set and intelligence, enabling horse and rider to cross-over and win in a spectrum of equine disciplines while avoiding the old cliché – "Jack of all trades and master of none."

Katrina and Dualin Dude performing dressage with the Southern Eventing and Dressage Association (SEDA).

The Stock Horse is indeed a master of its realm and seemingly endless performance capabilities which has contributed to its moniker: "One Horse, Three Events - reining, cutting, cow horse and whatever else you want to do."

The author's students and Wind River Ranch stock regularly crossover into other disciplines totally unrelated to the cow horse industry, i.e., dressage, Western pleasure, Western riding, halter, trail, barrel racing, etc.

The first photo in this chapter clearly depicts one such example of Some Hot Chic; a money earner in reined cow horse with the National Reined Cow Horse Association and the Louisiana Stock Horse Association, winning the coveted Triple Crown, consisting of reining, cutting and cow horse events. The mare is also a point earner, Champion and Circuit Champion in amateur reining and cow horse with the American Quarter Horse Association as well as a money earner and Champion in barrel racing.

Another example of the reined cow horses' athletic ability is seen in the following photo of Dualin Dude, a 2005 AQHA chestnut gelding, by the Wind River Ranch Stallion Dualin Oak and out of Stella Peaches. This gelding was bred, started, trained and shown by the author at the Wind River Ranch.

Dualin Dude is a Champion and money earner in reining, cutting and cow horse as well as being successfully shown and placing in six other events.

In addition to Dualin Dude being shown in the three-phase requirements of the reined cow horse: reining cutting and cow horse, the colt also has been shown in dressage, Western pleasure, Western riding, halter, ranch versatility and team sorting.

The author attributes this phenomena to the Stock Horse's breeding and its training in the old style or Vaquero (Spanish) training methods and equipment which produces a horse that's well disciplined, broke, light in the face and can be controlled with a whisper at the end of the horses training.

Reining trainers look for the Stock Horse Breeding for the athletic ability, big stops, heart and great minds. Cutters look for the same attributes but add another quality of the Stock horse: superior cow sense.

Allison Granier and Rudy. Team Sorting Champions and money earners.

As one great California icon and Stock Horse breeder once told the author, "Some folks buy my horses to be a reining horse, others want a cutting horse but most want a reined cow horse. Basically, whatever they want my horses for, the horse can do it".

The following photo depicts Dualin Dude being shown by the author in cutting:

Rick and Dualin Dude Cutting waiting for the cows to separate to begin cutting.

Overall, if you're just entering the performance horse industry and you have a limited amount of funds to invest in a multiple-event performance horse, the logical choice would be the purchase of a reined cow horse. With due diligence and care, this breed of horse will provide you with many years of enjoyable service, enhance your winning and showing capability and earn your respect with each cross-over discipline you subject it to. There are many breeds of horses to choose from but in the end of it all, the reined cow horse will remain, "King of The Cow Horses!"

"Until Next Time, Keep 'Em Between The Bridle!"